Hamburg Law Review
2018/2

Hamburg Law Review

Towards Use of the UNIDROIT Principles 2016 in Practice – a Bridge between Common and Civil Law

Law Review of the
Faculty of Law
at the University of Hamburg

Editors in Chief:
Eckart Brödermann
Hinrich Julius
Marian Paschke

Editors of this Issue:
Eckart Brödermann
Marian Paschke

2018/2

Subscription Information for the journal Hamburg Law Review
ISSN 2511-3933

Electronic Edition
An electronic edition of this journal is available
at most European online stores
ISBN electronic edition 978-3-7494-0241-0

Purchase information regarding
this issue of the journal as a separate book
ISBN print edition 978-3-7494-9295-4

Production
Books on Demand GmbH
In de Tarpen 42
22848 Norderstedt
Tel.: +49 40 – 53 43 35 80
Fax: +49 40 – 53 43 35 84
Email: joerg.zaag@bod.de
URL: www.bod.de

Content

Towards Use of the UNIDROIT Principles 2016 in Practice – a Bridge between Common and Civil Law

On September 13, 2018, the University of Hamburg was one of the supporters of an international arbitration conference including a faculty from over 20 nations. It was organized at the occasion of the 10th anniversary of the Chinese European Arbitration Center (www.ceac-arbitration.com). In its session, the delegates discussed options to bridge between common and civil law. Regarding the choice of the applicable contractual regime for a contract, in combination with an arbitration clause, the delegates discussed the risk reducing and cost saving tool of the UNIDROIT Principles of International Commercial Contracts 2016.

This volume of the Hamburg Law Review bundles the opening speech of Prof. Markus Kotzur at the University of Hamburg, followed by an analysis from Prof. Bruno Zeller (Crawley, Australia) of article 35 of the CEAC Hamburg Arbitration Rules (which explicitly incentivizes to choose the UNIDROIT Principles or the CISG on a stand-alone basis or the CISG in combination with the UNIDROIT Principles). Further contributions include articles from Gerhard Wegen/Benedikt Keil (Suttgart, Germany), Roger Barton (New York, USA) and Rina See/Dharshini Prasad (London, England) who all describe the feasibility to use the UNIDROIT Principles in practice against the background of the laws in their respective jurisdictions. This volume ends with a vivid summary of the discussions by Anish Wadia (Mumbai, India) and Magdalena Göbel (Hamburg, Germany).

The editors hope that, with this edition, they can contribute to the distribution of the UNIDROIT Principles 2016 around the globe.

Eckart Brödermann   Marian Paschke

Introductory Greetings

Dear Professor Paschke, dear Professor Mankowski, dear Professor Bröderman, dear organizers, esteemed guests from all over the world, ladies and gentlemen,

welcome to Hamburg, welcome to our law faculty, welcome to the Conference "International Arbitration in the light of the Belt and Road Initiative: Building Bridges – Building Connections." It is also my great pleasure to extend a warm welcome from our Dean, Professor Tilman Repgen, who is unfortunately not able to be here this afternoon but strongly supports the conference´s aims and spirit and wishes your scientific encounters great success. You could not have chosen a better time to visit Hamburg – this month the city celebrates "China time". You could not have chosen a better venue for your pre-conference. Our faculty coordinates one of the most important projects in European-Chinese legal dialogue, the China-EU law school, a Chinese-European scientific as well as educational joint venture located in Beijing. Under our faculty´s aegis, 16 top universities and 28 research institutes as well as major law firms from both China and Europe implement degree programs, research projects, and continuing education courses. There could be no better proof that we take seriously what also the founders of the faculty in 1919 had aimed to achieve: understanding law in its international contexts. By the way, how about a re-visit for our 100th anniversary next year? Be welcome! Finally, you could not have chosen a better motto for the pre-conference: "building bridges – building connections".

When the Belt and Road Initiative was first introduced by President Xi Jinping in 2013, building bridges and building connections was doubtlessly one on the new policy´s demanding objectives. And doubtlessly, too, there were more skeptical voices that raised concerns whether the ancient Silk Route´s grand tradition was too ambitious a model for a 21st Century follow-up. The Chinese President was maybe encouraged by a famous Confucius-quote that might also inspire us: "When it is obvious that the goals cannot be reached, don't adjust the goals, adjust the action steps."

And adjusted they are. The initiative, referring to the land-based "Silk Road Economic Belt" and the seagoing "21st Century Maritime Silk Road" extends to over 60 countries in Asia, Europe, Africa and Oceania. It aims to increase connectivity and economic development for countries along the route through infrastructure projects that will promote the movement of goods, services, information and people. This is all the more remarkable in times in which free trade policies are – to put it mildly – under increased scrutiny and not unreservedly supported by countries any more for which free trade seemed to be a natural part of their political DNA. China wants to strengthen its role as global financial center and promote the internationalization of the yuan through yuan-denominated projects and yuan loans. The initiative not only creates opportunities for Public-Private Partnerships (PPP), joint partnerships between International and Chinese companies, as well as access to cheap funding through a number of financing institutions but it demands European answers, too. Your conference will for sure provide possible answers related to a very specific but very relevant field: international arbitration in the "Belt and Road"-initiative´s context. Imaging that the overall project value is estimated at 1 trillion USD, the legal as well as economic impact of potentially upcoming arbitration procedures is beyond question. Extensive infrastructure investments with roads, railways, bridges, ports in over 60 countries are planned. The reduction of physical and regulatory barriers, connected routes and simplified processes displays the vison of a "globalization 2.0". Economic globalization, regional integration through investments, joint development and growth, and shared harvesting of the economic fruits shall go hand in hand. All that shall be accompanied by politics of multilateralism, regional cooperation, alignment of interests, strengthening of political ties through interdependence and connectivity. Law, Politics and Economics dare their Eurasian dreams.

Talking about arbitration as a dispute resolution mechanism, however, means addressing much more than law, politics and economics. It means addressing trust. Trust in a system of legal, political and economic interaction requires adequate means for the resolution of unavoidably arising disputes. It is a happy coincidence that this year´s Chinese Year of the Dog symbolizes loyalty, mutual trust and compatibility – exactly the same values on which the Belt and Road-Initiative is based upon. If memoranda of understandings are signed between the Chinese European Arbitration Center in Hamburg and the Thailand Arbitration Center, furthermore between the Chinese European Arbitration Center and the Cairo Regional Center for International Commercial Arbitration, this is a sign of trust. Our faculty is very privileged to host the official signing and pre-conference. In course of the next two days, you got plenty things to discuss and I wish you fruitful discussion. Confucius again might provide guidance: "To rule a country of a thousand chariots, there must be reverent attention to business, and sincerity; economy in expenditure, and love for men".

Thank you.

Markus Kotzur

The Chinese Silk Road – A Need to Rethink Dispute Resolution Choices?

Bruno Zeller*

I. Introduction

The One Road One Belt (OBOR or now BRI) initiative also referred to as China's "Silk Road" initiative, involves so far, an unprecedented $900 billion plan to supercharge trade channels between China and Europe, and its neighbours in the west.[1] It will herald a "new era of globalization" as the proposed rail, sea and road link will connect Central Asia, the Middle East and Europe.[2]

Not all countries – some are major trading nations - are either included in the initiative or are cautious, the United States in particular. They are taking a sceptical stance towards China's international engagement and deeper economic ties in more generally the Asia Pacific region. Whatever the views might be, the reality is that the project is not faltering and in effect a closer economic tie between China and Europe is inevitable as it arguably has the potential to specifically benefit both parties.
Indeed, the economic competitiveness of all participants in this project will be greatly enhanced. However, the unfortunate issue - which still has not been resolved satisfactorily - is that the legal differences between parties is still at odds with the economic

---

* Dr. Bruno Zeller is a Professor of Transnational Law in the Law School at the University of Western Australia, Perth, Adjunct Professor, School of Law, Murdoch University Perth and the Sir Zelman Cowen Centre, Victoria University, Melbourne, Fellow of the Australian Institute for Commercial Arbitration, Panel of Arbitrators – MLAANZ, Visiting Professor Stetson Law School, Florida, Humboldt University Berlin and Aalborg University, Denmark.

[1] http://knowledge.wharton.upenn.edu/article/can-chinas-one-belt-one-road-initiative-match-the-hype/
[2] See generally
https://www.aph.gov.au/About_Parliament/Parliamentary_Departments/Parliamentary_Library/pubs/BriefingBook45p/ChinasRoad

seamless trade efforts. This issue arguably is one of the drawbacks of free trade agreements which regulate at the border legal issues but not beyond. As the Silk Road is not a free trade agreement the creation of a mechanism permitting the establishment of a transnational alternative legal system is possible as the process is not driven by governments but by contractual parties. This effort hinges on the choice of arbitration as a dispute resolution mechanism which is one step toward transnational law implementations and hence predictability. This is so as dispute resolution clauses not only contain a choice of a forum but also a governing substantial law. This is especially helpful as many legal systems specifically in central Asia are not very well known and hence foster uncertainty.

To that end the Chinese European Arbitration Centre (CEAC) in Hamburg is well placed to be playing an important role in shaping the dispute resolution landscape within the new emerging global trade due to its novel construction of the choice of the governing law rules. Indeed, Paul Hayes at the Kuala Lumpur International Arbitration week in 2017 noted that arbitration needs to be rethought on the One Belt One Road regime.[3]

As there is no total uniformity among the leading institutional arbitration rules, a carful choice needs to be made by contract drafters. There is no doubt CEAC has to view the Singapore International Arbitration Centre (SIAC) as its closest rival in being the dominant force in the arbitration sphere in Asia. The Queen Mary University of London International Arbitration Survey which was released on 9 May 2018 "ranked SIAC as the most preferred in Asia and 3rd out of the top 5 arbitral institutions in the world"[4]. This fact must be counterbalanced by the problem that enforcements of foreign judgment in China remains difficult.[5] However the enforceability of judgements from Hong Kong in China gives the Hong Kong Arbitration Centre a unique

---

[3] http://www.39essex.com/content/wp-content/uploads/2017/05/2017-KLIAW-OBOR-Harmonisation-of-Arbitration-Rules-PJHayes-3rd.pdf
[4] Press Release by CIAC May 10, 2018. On file with author.
[5] *Moser, M.* Dispute Resolution in China (JurisNet 2012) 381.

advantage. [6] An enforcement agreement between Hong Kong and China was concluded in 2006 and in 2008 it was reinforced through the Mainland Judgement Ordinance (Cap. 597).[7]

In addition, anecdotally the argument has been advanced not only by the Chinese Government but also by some in the legal profession that CIETAC appears to be the preferred arbitration forum a far as Chinese companies are concerned. To support arbitration, the Supreme People's Court of China has, in its Opinion on Providing Judicial Services and Safeguards for the Building of One Belt One Road by People's Courts (OBOR Opinion) issued in July 2015, specifically indicated support towards the use of international commercial and maritime arbitration for resolving cross-border disputes arising from the OBOR Initiative.[8] However, this needs to be balanced with the effect of the rules issued by the PRC State Council on November 19, 2010 which increase the scrutiny over foreign representative offices, and enhance supervision on the activities, and impose more stringent compliance requirements. The Administrative Rules on Registration of Representative Offices of Foreign Enterprises (the new rules) took effect March 1, 2011.[9] In addition it must be kept in mind that an arbitrator must be chosen from a list prepared by CIETAC art. 13(2).[10] This still leaves enforcement of judgments in China in a tentative state.

From a European point of view the very purpose of the creation of CEAC was its focus "on world-wide arbitration matters, which have a direct or indirect tie to China."[11] Considering the

---

[6] *King Fung Tsang*, Hong Kong's Role in OBOR dispute resolutions in Sooksripaisarnkit, P. & Garimella, R. China's One Belt one Road Initiative and Private International Law, 200.

[7] Ibid 201 and 202.

[8] http://en.pkulaw.cn/display.aspx?cgid=251003&lib=law document number No. 9 [2015] of the Supreme People's Court **Date issued**: 06-16-2015, **Effective date**: 06-16-2015.

[9] https://www.chinabusinessreview.com/rules-further-tighten-regulation-of-foreign-representative-offices/

[10] http://hk.lexiscn.com/asiapg/articles/cietac-arbitration-procedures-and-appointment-of-an-arbitrator.html

[11] *Brödermann E.*, The Impact of the INIDROIT Principles on International Contract and Arbitration Practice – the Experience of a German Lawyer. Unif. L. Rev. Vol XVI 2011-3, 589 at 606.

importance of OBOR it can be argued that any country along the supply line has at least indirect ties with China hence is within the contemplation of CEAC.

This paper will demonstrate that on balance CEAC is the most versatile of all the mentioned rules as its governing law article 35 is the outstanding rule which is superior to other rules.

The importance of this paper is based on the question of how a dispute resolution finds its best "safe harbour". The procedural rules as well as the substantive rules must allow for the greatest choice to adjust a contract to the needs of trading parties and hence minimise perceived risks. This is best done by a choice of law which is acceptable to both parties and transnational laws could and will achieve that goal.

This paper therefore will discuss two points. First the utility of article 35 of the CEAC rules and secondly - and only as far as needed - the utility of the CISG and the UNIDROIT Principles (UPICC) to create a common transnational climate to overcome the well-known civil-common law divide.

As far as the first point is concerned, the issue of having a valid arbitral award enforced in another jurisdiction within the Silk Road participants is of paramount importance. This is facilitated as the CEAC rules embrace the use of uniform legal instruments and are not simply relying on domestic black letter law and secondly, as noted already, article 35 suggests that the governing law is best suited to a multi-jurisdictional legal climate which is prevalent within the Silk Road.

Importantly the biggest participants in the Silk Road, namely the EU and China, are both signatories to the CISG, and China and many States of the EU are members of the UNIDROIT Governing Council. Arguably therefore from a political point of view both instruments are known in the EU and China. However, the real problem is - and remains - that the contract drafters are not familiar with international instruments and rather rely on a domestic black letter law. Bortolotti noted that "most lawyers refuse even to consider this alternative, because they uncritically accept, as an undisputed dogma, that only a domestic law can offer sufficient certainty and foreseeability."[12]

The CEAC rules also wisely allow for this rather sometimes unfortunate choice of law. What can be said is that at least a conversation or a recognition of viable alternatives between the "traditionalists" and the more progressive contract drafters will be created. But most importantly CEAC attempts to influence international arbitration drafters to recognise the value or at least think of the value of the CISG and UPICC. Gordon and Rosett noted that "[I]f nobody knows that [transnational instruments are] there, the law has little capacity to shape behaviour."[13]

As to the second point, a discussion on the main differences between the civil and common law on the utility of the CISG and UPICC will highlight its importance as currently only the United Kingdom is connected to the Silk Road. Australia, India and importantly the United States are merely on the sideline. However, U.S. and English law is still an important choice of law in arbitration and hence this difference must be noted.

II. Article 35: The Applicable law

It is argued that article 35 which regulates the applicable governing law reflects and accommodates the various legal systems along the Silk Road and brings the economic and legal landscapes into the same orbit. Hayward already in 2015 noted the uniqueness of CEAC in general. He observed:
The Chinese European Arbitration Centre, having a particular (though not exclusive) focus on the resolution of Sino – European business disputes, has tailored its model arbitration

---

[12] *Bortolotti, F.* Towards a Transnational Commercial Law: The Essential Role of the UNIDROIT Principles. In UNIDROIT (ed) Eppur si muove: The Age of Uniform Law, Essays in Honour of Michael Joachim Bonell to celebrate his 70th birthday (2016), 1258, at 1262.

[13] *Gordon, J. and Rosett, A.*, in Bonell, M.J. (ed) A New Approach to International Commercial Contracts, (Kluwer Law) (1999), 388.

clause and also integrated three specific features into its institutional rules in light of this context.[14]

Article 35 in full notes the following important points:
The arbitral tribunal shall apply the law or rules of law designated by the parties as applicable to the substance of the dispute. The parties may wish to consider the use of this model clause with the following option by marking one of the following boxes: This contract shall be governed by

a) the law of the jurisdiction of _____ [country to be inserted], or

b) the United Nations Convention on Contracts for the International Sale of Goods of 1980 (CISG) without regard to any national reservation, supplemented for matters which are not governed by the CISG, by the UNIDROIT Principles of International Commercial Contracts and these supplemented by the otherwise applicable national law, or

c) the UNIDROIT Principles of International Commercial Contracts supplemented by the otherwise applicable law.

In the absence of any such agreement, the arbitral tribunal shall apply the rules of law which it determines to be appropriate.

As noted, CEAC suggested several options in the choice of the substantive law. Each one will be discussed briefly in order to understand the interconnectedness and the utility of transnational law in a new economic landscape created by the Silk Road. It should also be mentioned that article 35 was inspired or took guidance from the suggested Model Clauses of UPICC which indicates the strong transnational character of CEAC.

---

[14] *B. Hayward*, Arbitral Discretion in Resolving Conflicts of Laws - The Case for a Bright-Line Closest Connection Test in International Commercial Arbitration (PhD Thesis, Monash University, 2015), 547.

1. The law of a jurisdiction

Anecdotally it has been noted that the dispute resolution mechanism is called the midnight clause as it is often the last issue which is included after lengthy negotiations and hence it is not always the best choice. Hayes specifically noted:

More thought needs to be given by parties to the 'one minute to midnight' disputes clause when finalising OBOR contracts. With whom does the bargaining power truly rest here? Is China really going to risk losing a vital cog in the OBOR project over a disputes clause?[15]

The answer is probably no. However, the principle of good business where everybody makes profit is very important to China and anywhere else for that matter. Hence a proper jurisdiction clause is the first step towards good business relationships.

It is not unusual that the law of a particular jurisdiction gives rise to problems unless both parties are familiar with the chosen law. As an example, in commodity sales English law is often chosen because of its long history dealing with maritime law. However, it also poses problems as foreign legal experts need to be consulted. In addition, many lawyers are not familiar with legal transplantation and often are "lured" into a governing law which favors one party. As an example, if a Turkish party would suggest that a neutral law ought to be chosen namely Swiss law they in fact have chosen their own law. Turkey transplanted the Swiss law of Obligation into their own domestic landscape. The point is – as Bortolotti noted:

Experienced lawyers know how difficult it is really to understand a foreign law even when it is easy to access its source, which is not always the case.[16]

---

[15] http://www.39essex.com/content/wp-content/uploads/2017/05/2017-KLIAW-OBOR-Harmonisation-of-Arbitration-Rules-PJHayes-3rd.pdf
[16] *Bortolotti* above n 12, at 1263

This is specifically so in Common Law where many principles are to be found in jurisprudence and not statutes. However, through a selection of a domestic law the CISG might still be enlivened as it has been ratified and is part of the domestic law.

Unfortunately, there are many instances where counsels were not aware of this issue and argued the case wrongly based – as in *Ginza Pte Ltd v Vista Corp Pty Ltd* - on common law principles.[17] Unlike the Australian courts, the New Zealand High Court understood the interrelationship of the application of the CISG and hence the interpretative mandate. In *RJ & AM Smallmon v. Transport Sales Limited and Grant Alan Miller*[18] French J noted that the CISG applies but that "Counsel for both parties nevertheless sought to rely on domestic sale of goods law. However, in my view, recourse to domestic law is prohibited by Article 7"[19] French J went on to explain that:

The requirement imposed by Article 7(1) namely to have regard "to the international character of the convention and to the need to promote uniformity in application" is generally accepted as establishing what has been called a principle of autonomous interpretation. That means the Convention must be applied and interpreted exclusively on its own terms, having regard to the principles of the Convention and Convention-related decisions in overseas jurisdictions. Recourse to domestic case law is to be avoided.[20]

The court also refereed to academic writing[21] and did correct council who attempted to justify the use of domestic law by referring to article 7(2). French J stated that article 7(2) "only authorises reference to domestic law in order to fill gaps in interpretation."[22]

---

[17] See for example editorial comments in *Ginza Pte Ltd v Vista Corp Pty Ltd* .
    http://cisgw3.law.pace.edu/cases/030117a2.html
[18] New Zealand 30 July 2010 High Court of New Zealand (*RJ & AM Smallmon v. Transport Sales Limited and Grant Alan Miller*) [http://cisgw3.law.pace.edu/cases/100730n6.html].
[19] ibid.
[20] Ibid.
[21] P Schlechtriem, *Requirements of Application and Sphere of Applicability of the CISG* (2005) 36 VUWLR 781 at 789-790.
[22] *RJ & AM Smallmon v. Transport Sales Limited and Grant Alan Miller*, Above n.

In addition, there is always a chance that the arbitral tribunal can resort to apply the rules of law which it determines to be appropriate. Professor Brödermann notes one example where this eventuated namely the proposal of the Chairman of a Swiss arbitration, in 2001, and again in 2017 upon proposal of the respondent in a CEAC arbitration, in order to avoid research and proof of otherwise applicable Chinese law to European arbitrators.[23]

Importantly the CEAC rules also note in article 18 that the seat of the arbitration will be Hamburg, unless the parties have agreed otherwise. The significance of the seat on the arbitral process has been described in *C v D*[24] as having been considered in a number of recent authorities.

The effect of them is that the agreement as to the seat of an arbitration is akin to agreement to an exclusive jurisdiction clause. Not only is there agreement to the arbitration itself but also to the courts of the seat having supervisory jurisdiction over that arbitration. By agreeing to the seat, the parties agree that any challenge to an interim or final award is to be made only in the courts of the place designated as the seat of the arbitration.[25]

For the purpose of this paper it is sufficient to note that the underlying reason is that arbitration is connected to a legal system and hence to the procedural rules of that system. A choice of a seat will determine which legal system is relevant in assisting the arbitration process. It goes without saying that the *lex arbitri* is not a universal law as it can differ from one jurisdiction to another. In this case German and where necessary EU law will be the relevant applicable system of law. This is of added importance as the seat should be outside of China at all costs, as a way of avoiding possible problems in relation to Chinese courts and their oversight and control of the arbitral process.

---

[23] http://arbitrationblog.kluwerarbitration.com/2018/03/25/future-cross-border-contracts-combination-arbitration-clauses-unidroit-principles-international-commercial-contracts-provide-practice-proven-bridge-common-civil/
[24] Lloyd's Law Report [2007] Vol 2, 367.
[25] Ibid at 375.

Hayward does argue that the seat being identified as Hamburg, with any other indicated place (including Chinese places) presumed to be a venue for oral hearings only. However,CEAC specifically advises against the choice of a mainland Chinese seat, and even (out of caution) mainland China as a venue for oral hearings.[26] The problem which could emerge is that an award can be susceptible to a review in China with the possible exception of a Hong Kong seated arbitration.

In sum considering that the trade within OBOR has a very long and possibly complicated supply line and hence crossing several jurisdictions and legal systems, the choice of any specific legal system will not be the best available choice. It simply does not minimize the risk of having to deal with a legal system which is not understood or best suited to the circumstances. The exception of course is an institutional rule like the CEAC rules. The problem which unfortunately even a well drafted rule like article 35 cannot overcome is – should the CISG have been applicable – it could have been excluded which unfortunately is still routinely done.

It is argued that the astute contract drafter would include either options (b) or (c) of article 35 as it fits best in the transnational way to do business. This is specially so with the eventual "trade fusion" between China and Europe. A strong convincing argument is the fact that UPICC has found its way into several legal systems. Of Importance in relation to OBOR is that Germany, France and other EU nations and China have embraced and understood the importance of UPICC in their modernization of contract law.[27]

---

[26] *Hayward. B.* above n 14, at 546.
[27] See *J.A. Estrella-Faria*, The Influence of the UNIDROIT Principles of International Commercial Contracts on National Law, in UNIDROIT (ed) Eppur si muove: The Age of Uniform Law, Essays in Honour of Michaela Joachim Bonell to celebrate his 70th birthday (2016), 1318 ff.

2. The CISG and the UNIDROIT Principles – their significance in international trade.

a) Introduction

To fully appreciate the choice of law as noted in article 35 (b) and (c) of either the CISG or UPICC or a combination thereof requires explanations in order for arbitral parties to make a considered and informed choice. As a general point, the CISG has been ratified by 89 countries with the notable exception of the United Kingdom and India. Most of the Central Asian countries as well as China and most of the EU countries have ratified the Convention. Hence the CISG as such is a useful uniform law when dealing with countries along the Silk Road.

The starting point in understanding the significance of uniform instruments is an observation made by Professor Kronke who noted:
What we see looking at the two instruments – the CISG as the mother of all modern conventions on the law of specific contracts and the UPICC as the (inevitably) soft-law source of modern general contract law – are neither competitors nor apples and pears. What we see is actually, and even more, potentially, a fruitful coexistence … [T]he UNIDROIT Contract Principles are, obviously, complementary in that they address a wide range of topics of general contract law which neither the CISG nor any other existing or future convention devoted to a specific type of transaction would ever venture to touch upon.[28]

Professor Kronke importantly highlighted the advantages of the interplay between both instruments. As the CISG is a convention it takes precedent over UPICC - a model law - or as Professor Bergsten noted an "international restatement of general principles of contract law."[29]

---

[28] *Herbert Kronke*, The UN Sales Convention, the UNIDROIT Contract Principles and the Way Beyond, 25 J.L. & Com. 451, at 458-59.

[29] *Bergsten E.*, Foreword in John Felemegas (ed), An International Approach to the Interpretation of the United Nations Convention on Contracts for the International Sale of Goods (1980) as Uniform Sales Law in Cambridge University Press, at X.

As noted above there are many advantages but also some disadvantages in the choice of the CISG and UPICC. As an example, where strict compliance is required – that is the slightest deviation gives rise to a breach – the CISG or UPICC can resolve the issues but English law is preferred such as in commodity sales. However, it is argued that all contracts if so desired can be successfully governed by transnational laws. The most important point is that the contract drafters must understand why such a choice has been made and what risks are specifically to be covered by the contractual terms.

b) The application of the CISG in conjunction with UPICC

Two preliminary comments are warranted, First the problem and the strength of the CISG is that it is a treaty and hence had to be drafted in a way:
to encourage adoption by various states, to create a high comfort level with the appropriateness of the instrument, [and hence] there is a strong tendency toward the creation of instruments that will reflect the legal traditions and existing rules of the potential adopting states.[30]

The drafters of UPICC on the other hand were not obliged to support and defend their respective domestic law, hence the instrument can attempt to strive towards a goal of balance and fairness.[31] Arguably therefore to combine the two instruments into one contract would enhance the quality and hence predictability of an international contractual relationships.

Secondly the discussion below assumes that the choice of the otherwise applicable law is a "CISG country" as otherwise a problem might arise. The issue is that the CISG has now lost the "mantle of a treaty" and must be viewed simply as a model

---

[30] *Gabriel, H.,* Using the Model Clauses for the UNIDROIT Principles as the Basis for Getting the Principles in Arbitrations and Courts Seventh Annual Transnational Law Teachers Conference Washington D.C. November 17-18, 2016. On file with author.

[31] Ibid.

law. This in itself is not a problem as there is ample case material as well as literature and hence "for the purpose of understanding the provisions one would not feel left out in the woods at night."[32] However the task of UPICC now is only to fill the gaps in the CISG. Professor Gabriel states the problem in the following way:

[to only fill the gaps] requires one to determine what the CISG is. Is it the text alone or is it the text as understood by the legions of interpretations that already exist? For if it is the latter, what is left to interpret? And even if it is the former, there is an interpretation in and of itself of what the text of the CISG alone says.[33]

This issue might get complicated, but this observation might not be useful in practice but ought to be kept in mind. No doubt experienced arbitrators would be able to overcome this perceived hurdle.

Hence the first observation is that the CISG is not a contract law as it is a sales law and in addition it only governs the formation of the contract and the rights and obligations of the contractual parties arising from such a contract.[34] As such it is not a code and contains exclusions such as noted in article 4 namely that the CISG is not concerned with the validity of the contract.

The starting point to understand the interrelationship between the two instruments starts with article 6 of the CISG which allows a party to either exclude or derogate from or vary the effects of any of the provisions within the Convention. It reflects the general principle of freedom of contract. As Borisova correctly noted that it creates the climate "within which the contracting parties have the freedom to act in conformity with their business interests."[35] In combining the two instruments UPICC is in a sense the "glue" that holds the contract together.

---

[32] Ibid.

[33] Ibid.

[34] Article 4 CISG.

[35] *Borisova, B.,* Freedom of contract: Remarks on the manner in which the UNIDROIT Principles may be used to interpret or supplement Article 6 of the CISG. In John Felemegas (ed), An International Approach to the Interpretation of the United Nations Convention on Contracts for the International Sale of Goods (1980) as Uniform Sales Law in Cambridge University Press, at 39.

The task of UPICC is noted in article 7 of the CISG which explains that matters not expressly settled in the CISG "must be "settled in conformity with the general principles on which it is based." As UPICC has been based on the same general principles as the CISG it can be used to assist in determining and elaborating on the general principles. Hence it will strengthen the understanding of the application of general principles. Most importantly though article 7 also notes that in the absence of such principles recourse to the otherwise applicable domestic law needs to be applied. However, UPICC will replace the domestic law, hence the advantage in effect is that all substantive issues can be resolved without the need to revert to the otherwise governing law except of course if there is a mandatory law which becomes applicable.

In essence a truly transnational application and interpretation of the contract is achieved which is based on fairness which "protects the weaker party from the dominant's party behaviour and thus guarantees the equality of both contracting parties."[36] This is achieved as neither of the domestic laws are used hence a fair playing field has been created favouring neither of the two parties.

The problem which can has arisen is that a court or arbitrator mistakenly resorted to domestic rules that is followed the "homeward trend" instead of applying the CISG correctly. As demonstrated above it is argued that the inclusion of UPICC will reduce the temptation as UPICC needs to be addressed and hence the question of applying domestic law is reduced. A point which will be disused below is the importance of correctly applying the terms of the contract hence following the correct interpretative mandate and hence a court or tribunal must be careful not to overstep "the mark" as otherwise article 7 and 8 CISG would be breached. The first step in overcoming this problem is of course overcome by the inclusion of UPICC as allowed in article 35 CEAC. In addition, CEAC rules also allow for the application of UPICC on its own.

---

[36] ibid at 41.

c) The application of UPICC

An important point needs to be noted at the beginning. The argument against the use of UPICC which has been advanced is that the Principles are not widely used and secondly, they are not a "law", only a model law. Professor Gabriel argues that both the arguments miss the point. The real question which needs to be asked is whether:

the Principles are in and of themselves, good rules, based on the content of the Principles and not their current usage. For if they become the new international commercial standards, either by custom and usage within commercial transactions or by direct adoption by a jurisdiction, both of these concerns disappears."[37]

However soft laws in general have been successful because they are not binding. In effect it does not pose any threat to a national legal system because it is "left to legislatures, courts and arbitral tribunals to decide to what extent they assist in the solution of problems."[38]

Given the above, the application of UPICC as the governing law raises two points; first - and not a contentious issue – what effects does UPICC exert on a contract if it is the governing principles? This is not a difficult question as UPICC - being a model law – takes on the mantle of the governing contractual terms between the parties. The effect is that the otherwise governing law only applies to cover any possible gaps or overrules UPICC if there is a mandatory law in place.

Secondly as UPICC has had several amendments and hence like with Incoterms it is prudent to include the relevant version into the contract and in this case the suggestion that the 2016 version should be used.

It must also be recognised that it is near impossible for any lawyer to know fully or understand domestic law even if they are

---

[37] *Gabriel, H.* above no. 30.
[38] *Goode R.,* "Communication on European Contract Law", cited in GOPALAN S., "New Trends in the Making of International Commercial Law", Journal of Law and Commerce 2004, pp. 117-168.

practicing in the EU. Hence the question which should be asked is: what system can give more certainty and ease of understanding in a global world? Professor Brödermann in relation to UPICC noted:

Most of the 211 principles constitute a compromise between different approaches to a given contractual topic, while others reflect a universal understanding or an emerging general principle of law.[39]

Hence "by their nature, [UPICC] is similar to most national laws."[40] It follows that an astute contract drafter therefore would recognise that UPICC is at least an excellent template and any articles can be replaced or modified to suite specific risks or trade practices. Arguably because the comprise between different approaches has been reached time and energy will be reduced and a "personalised" trade relationship can be created by overcoming legal barriers.

The importance in "personalising" the trade relationships - which is an important feature in Asia – is the fact that the divide between the common law and civil law is not an issue any more.

d) In the absence of any agreement

A brief comment ought to be made in relation to the option of the tribunal to select a rule of law in the absence of a choice by the parties. Considering that article 35 specifically notes a "rule of law" and given the dominance of the CISG and UPICC it is more than likely that a tribunal would chose UPICC. Arguably this is so as the tribunal would always strive to make sure that the strict application does not lead to an inequitable result in the dispute at hand.

---

[39] See http://arbitrationblog.kluwerarbitration.com/2018/03/25/future-cross-border-contracts-combination-arbitration-clauses-unidroit-principles-international-commercial-contracts-provide-practice-proven-bridge-common-civil/
[40] *Brödermann, E.,* above n 11, at 590.

III. The common law view on Transnational law

1. Introductory comments

It is useful to note that the CISG was constructed as a compromise between the civil and common law systems. As a result, differences between the two systems will, in some cases, present different solutions. For the purpose of this paper only two issues are of great importance. First the way common law countries have received the CISG and UPICC and secondly how the common law interprets and applies the two instruments with special regard to good faith.

It is noteworthy to remember the results of a survey published in the Uniform Law Review in 2011 where Lake reported that "the British survey illustrated a dismissive attitude towards UPICC."[41] In Australia Finn pointed out that the Government in 2011 introduced a discussion paper in relation to reforming contract law but despite over 50 submissions, the proposal collapsed.[42] The general view was that "while domestic contract law worked well enough, Australia's business community needed to be provided with better protection in international sales."[43] It is interesting to note this comment considering that the CISG has been ratified but unfortunately in most cases poorly applied. Arguably the legal profession has still not fully understood and used the CISG correctly little alone seriously embarking on an understanding and usage of UPICC.

---

[41] *Lake, S.,* An Empirical Study of the UNIDROIT Principles – International and British Responses, Unif. L. Rev. 2011, 673.
[42] *P. Finn,* The UNIDROIT Principles: The Australian Response, in UNIDROIT (ed) Eppur si muove: The Age of Uniform Law, Essays in Honour of Michaela Joachim Bonell to celebrate his 70th birthday (2016), 1384, 1390 and 1391.
[43] Ibid 1391.

2. The Interpretative mandate – The English perspective

Lake noted several comments from major law firms which simply dismissed the utility of UPICC. The views in general on the utility of UPICC can be summarised as being "completely irrelevant and worthless. [It is] a product of civil law systems."[44] It is interesting to note the discrepancy between the views of British academics such as Roy Goode and the governments participation on all international working groups on transnational law. The working group for the preparation of the 2016 edition of UPICC contained Sir Ramsay a former judge of the Courts of Justice. It appears that government participation in working groups and councils does not translate into either ratifying the CISG or acknowledging the importance of transnational instruments in global trade.

The most frequently raised objection appears to be in relation to good faith and fair dealing, a principle in UPICC as well as the CISG. In particular the fact that UPICC and the CISG admit pre-contractual negotiations as an aid to interpretation and hence as evidence was rejected in common law.

The view of English courts is best illustrated by comments in 2009 by the House of Lords:
Both the Unidroit Principles of International Commercial Contracts … provide that in ascertaining the "common intention of the parties", regard shall be had to prior negotiations: … The same is true of the United Nations Convention on Contracts for the International Sale of Goods (1980). But these instruments reflect the French philosophy of contractual interpretation, which is altogether different from that of English law.[45]

The court explained the English position by stating that:
English law, on the other hand, mixes up the ascertainment of intention with the rules of law by depersonalising the contracting parties and asking, not what their intentions actually were, but

---

[44] *Lake* above n 41, at 681

[45] *Chartbrook* Ltd and another v Persimmon Homes Ltd and another [2009] UKHL 38 at para 39.

what a reasonable outside observer would have taken them to be.[46]

The problem with this view is that a decision of a court could be contrary to what the combined intention of the parties was. This is especially so as in may circumstances the question evolves around the choice of words by the parties. McLauchlan asked the penetrating question: "Why allow evidence of the fact that the parties have "united in rejecting" a particular meaning but disallow evidence of the fact that the parties have united in accepting a particular meaning?"[47] Simply put there is no need to "depersonalise" the parties contracts. As the subjective intent produces evidence it will only be admitted if it is objectively proven under the CISG or UPICC.

To put it differently, the important point is that not the production of evidence, but that the veracity of the evidence is tested in a "depersonalised" fashion. Lord Steyn noted that the subjective intent has "upset the horses in the commercial paddock"[48] and that "possibly we are swimming against the tide."[49] Arguably it is trite to argue that subjective intent can mean anything else but "undisclosed" or "uncommunicated" intentions[50]. The important point which speaks against the parol evidence rule is that contractual parties do not dwell on the meaning of words when they intended to close a deal hence to look back and attempt to give a meaning to a term from the equally situated person's point of view lacks credibility, specially without examining the special understanding between the parties. In addition, it can also be argued that parties seldom include facts into a contract which both parties are fully acquainted with or was understood by both parties. They simply take it as "a given." Hence the parol evidence rule in these circumstances is of little utility.

---

[46] Ibid.

[47] *McLauchlan, D*, 'Common Assumptions and Contract Interpretation' (1997) 113 Law Quarterly Review 237, 242.

[48] *Steyn, J.*, "The Intractable Problem of the Interpretation of Legal Texts (2003) 24 Sydney Law Review 5, at 9.

[49] *Lord Steyn*, "The Intractable Problem of the Interpretation of :Legal Texts" *Sydney Law Review 5* (2003).

[50] *McLauchlan, D.*, Contract Interpretation: What is it About? Sydney Law Review (2009) vol 31.5 at 12.

3. The Interpretative mandate - The Australian perspective

In Australia the development was both similar and dissimilar at the same time. In the Federal Court judges like Allsop J were advocating the benefits of UPICC and the CISG. However, the Principles never took root and were only mentioned in passing or as an alternative which was not acted upon. As an example in *Franklins Pty Ltd v Metcash Trading Ltd* the court stated:
How parties later acted, probative of what they themselves thought their obligations were, is difficult to reconcile with the objective paradigm.

Of course, if another paradigm were to be put in place, no such difficulty would arise. For instance, Arts 4.1-4.3 of the UNIDROIT *Principles of International Commercial Contracts* (3rd Ed) gives a primary role to the ascertainment of the actual common intention of the parties:[51]
Alsop J went on to note:
To a significant degree the approach to the construction and interpretation of contracts in the UNIDROIT Principles and the CISG reflects civil law principles: see Lord Hoffmann's comments in *Chartbrook Limited v Persimmon Homes Limited* http://www.bailii.org/uk/cases/UKHL/2009/38.html. This underlying difference in basal framework explains the brevity of the reference to the civil law by Lord Hoffmann in his discussion of the admissibility of pre-contractual negotiations in *Chartbrook Limited v Persimmon Homes Limited.*[52]

In essence the courts specially in Australia and to a lesser degree in England were aware of the usefulness but also differences between the CISG and UPICC and the parol evidence rule in the approach to the interpretation of contracts. In the end the court followed the well-known principles of the parol evidence rule and rejected or at least were not compelled to apply the subjective approach. Kirby J. in *Agricultural and Rural Finance Pty Ltd v Gardiner and Another*[53] argued as the

---

[51] *Franklins Pty Ltd v Metcash Trading Ltd* [2009] NSWCA 407 (16 December 2009) at para 6 and 7.
[52] Ibid at para 9.
[53] [2008] HCA 57.

dissenting judge that the contextual approach is now the standard way to give meaning to words in the course of statutory interpretation.[54] He rejected the view of the Appeal court which argued that "because the agreement was written by definition it had a meaning before any subsequent conduct of the parties."[55] Instead he argued:

I would not accept this conclusion as stating an absolute rule. I do not agree that later communications and conduct of parties to an agreement are inadmissible when tendered to indicate acceptance by the parties of a particular meaning of the language used in their agreement. [56]

Kirby J specifically argues in relation to the admissibility of post contractual conduct. However, the question is why is pre-contractual conduct not included in his argument? After all the true beginning of a construction of words and their meaning commences at the pre-contractual period, then progresses to a written statement and is followed by post contractual conduct. It is argued that all the "points" in the contractual life need to be reviewed as only then can a consistent meaning that is the true meaning, be elicited.

Corney pointed to an additional problem when approaching transnational law through the eyes of common law. He stated:

A particular English word used in an international convention may have a meaning different from the same word used in a domestic statute. It is not appropriate to apply prior domestic meaning to a word in a convention.[57]

To put it differently, the mandate of "international character" and "promote uniformity" has been interpreted by international jurisprudence as not reverting to domestic principles and jurisprudence but to consult international jurisprudence which can be found on the CISG Pace website.[58] The problem with

---

[54] Ibid at 115.
[55] Ibid.
[56] Ibid.
[57] *Corney, G.,* Mutant Stare Decisis; The Interpretation of Statutes which Incorporate International Treaties into Australian Law. [1994-95], 18 U. *Queensland L.J. 50,*at 58.
[58] See http://www.cisg.law.pace.edu

Australian jurisprudence is the fact that most of the Australian decisions are not correct but via the principle of precedent the errors have persisted.

However, the contextual approach is now widely used in Australia and giving Kirby the last word, he stated that "the interpretation of contracts is concerned as such with discovering the subjective intentions of writers of the words in question."[59]

4. The Interpretative mandate - The American Perspective

In the United States the usage of UPICC is somewhat different. The courts understood the applicability of UPICC. In *Koda v Carnival Corporations* the plaintiff argued that the court is compelled to address UPICC. Hoeveler DJ. in response pointed out that: "The Court took into consideration that the UNIDROIT Principles are not binding unless expressly provided for in a contract"[60] which they were not.

Generally speaking many courts in the United States were very familiar with the purpose and scope of UPICC which is best explained in *Ministry of Defence and Support v Cubic Defences*[61] where the court was asked to revisit a setting aside of an award under the New York Convention. The plaintiff argued that "reference to such international and equitable principles [such as UPICC] also violate Article V(1)(c) because this law exceeds the scope of the Terms of Reference."[62]

In response the court noted:
The Tribunal's reference to and application of the UNIDROIT Principles and principles such as good faith and fair dealing do not violate Article V(1)(c). The Tribunal applied these principles to differences contemplated by and falling within the terms of the

---

[59] *Kirby, M.*, Towards a Grand Theory of Interpretation: The Case of Statutes and Contracts.. *Statute law Review*, 24(2), 95, at 98.
[60] F.Supp.2d (2007), para 1.
[61] 29 F.Supp.2d 1168 (S.D.Cal. 1998).
[62] Ibid para [7].

submission to arbitration and therefore the Award does not violate Article V(1)(c).[63]

5. Article 8 CISG and the interpretative mandate

In sum it can be seen article 8 CISG is structured in two ways, first the subjective approach is to be used and only if it does not yield any result will the court use the objective approach. In essence the parol evidence rule is at odds with the contract interpretation of the CISG[64] and UPICC. The effect is that evidence which is admitted by using the subjective approach may not be admissible under the parol evidence rule. Most United States commentators comment that the parol evidence rule is inconsistent with the application of the CISG and by definition UPICC as well.[65] Gordly does argue that in "applying the parol evidence rule, a court should consider how reliable extrinsic evidence is likely to be."[66] He notes Posner who believed that:

The key is the distinction between what might be called 'objective' and 'subjective' evidence of ambiguity … By 'objective' evidence we mean that the evidence of ambiguity can be supplied by disinterested third parties … By 'subjective' evidence we mean the testimony of the parties themselves to what the contract means. 'Subjective' evidence is self-serving and easier to manufacture.[67]

The problem with this view is that no distinction has been drawn between the necessary proof which means that even a subjective view or evidence must be objectively proven. The whole criminal system relies on this notion. Also, even when a

---

[63] Ibid para[7].
[64] See generally *Bruno Zeller*, 'The Parol Evidence rule and the CISG – a Comparative Analysis' (2003) 36 *Comparative and International Law Journal of South Africa* 308.
[65] *J. Gordley*, The Parol Evidence Rule and Transnational Law: The CISG and the UNIDROIT Principles, in in UNIDROIT (ed) Eppur si muove: The Age of Uniform Law, Essays in Honour of Michael Joachim Bonell to celebrate his 70th birthday (2016), 1462, 1462 and 1463.
[66] Ibid at 1469.
[67] Ibd at 1469 and also fn 33.

disinterested third party looks at evidence they are still subject to personal views which are not objective but rather subjective.

The real issue is that the difference between the parol evidence rule - certainly as applied in England - and the transnational law is that the distinction between available evidence and the veracity of the evidence has been confused. It assumes that the disinterested third parties are objective and not prone to a view coloured by their own believes or how they view the evidence. Under the CISG and UPICC the subjective intent of the parties is still tested objectively by disinterested third parties that is judges or arbitrators. It is argued that the real and most important difference is that the transnational law allows more facts to be presented that is an arbitrator or judge needs to consider all of the relevant circumstances as an example noted in article 8 CISG and articles 4.1 *et seq.* UPICC for that matter.

The second point of the debate is that good faith is not a recognised principle in all common law jurisdictions which complicates the choice of a governing common law system. In England good faith is not applied whereas in the United States it is a principle embedded and explained in the Restatements. In Australia good faith is a principle in state courts but the High Court has not yet made definitive attempts as to its application. It must be admitted that the principle of good faith though recognised and being in existence has not been defined uniformly. It could even be argued that it is not capable to be defined. The work of Professors Summers[68] and Burton[69] warrants close attention. Especially Summers is of importance as his theory was the basis in explaining the application of good faith in article 205 in the second *Restatement of Contract* which appeared in 1979 (and was finally published in 1981).[70]

---

[68] See *Robert Summers*, The General Duty of Good Faith – its Recognition and Conceptualisation, 67(4) *Cornell L. Rev.* 810 (1982); *Robert Summers*, "Good Faith" in General Contract Law and the Sales Provision of the Uniform Commercial Code, 54 *Va. L. Rev.* 195 (1968).

[69] See *Steven Burton*, Breach of Contract and the Common Law Duty to Perform in Good Faith, 94 *Harv. L. Rev.* 369 (1980); *Steven Burton*, Good Faith Performance of a Contract within Article 2 of the Uniform Commercial Law Code, 67 *Iowa L. Rev.* 1 (1981); *Steven Burton*, More on Good Faith Performance of a Contract: A reply to Professor Summers, 69 *Iowa L. Rev.* 497 (1984).

[70] *Summers, R.*, General Duty of Good Faith, above n 68, at 810.

Summers theory basically relies on the excluder principle. He explains that the expression "good faith" as commonly (and sometimes vaguely) used by judges is best understood as an "excluder"; that is, it "has no general meaning or meanings of its own, but … serves to exclude many heterogeneous forms of bad faith."[71] However Burton provided arguably the best explanation of the use of good faith in interpreting contracts. He noted:

Good faith performance occurs when a party's discretion is exercised for any purpose within the reasonable contemplation of the parties at the time of formation – to capture opportunities that were preserved upon entering the contract, interpreted objectively.[72]

This paper argues that both the CISG and UPICC are in principle capable of accepting Burton's notion of good faith. It is completely within the spirit of the interpretive mandate of both instruments.

The very point is that specially Australia and England have not yet modernised the contract law in order to stay in step with current developments. Contract law is not an isolated area of law which in effect needs modernising as an analogues development has also been advocated by Dr. Hannah in cross border insolvency laws. He notes:

The ease with which larger Australian entitles can seek to use foreign laws in any restructuring through the recognition of such proceedings through the UNCITRAL Model Law on Cross-Border Insolvency means that the rationale for maintaining our present laws is not practically viable and that Australia's laws should be consistent with comparable nations and our trading partners.[73]

In sum, a similar if not identical argument can be made in relation to contract law specifically in the common law world. Reform is important and necessary as seen by many civil law

---

[71] *Summers*, "Good Faith" in General Contract Law, above n 68, at 196, 262.
[72] *Burton* above n 68. at 373.
[73] *N. Hannah*, A CASE FOR INSURANCE INSOLVENCY LAW REFORM IN AUSTRALIA, Australian Restructuring Insolvency & Turnaround Association Journal, March 2018, 30, at 34.

countries such as Germany who have undertaken the relevant reform and adjusted the domestic contract law to be more compatible with the transnational world. This reform has been undertaken by simply taking notice of UPICC.

IV. Conclusion

This paper has demonstrated that the Silk Road is posing new challenges in drafting a dispute resolution clause which will minimise the risks of non-enforcement of an arbitral award. In addition, it also has demonstrated that relying on a particular domestic jurisdiction is not the optimal solution. Importantly UPICC is increasingly finding its way into contracts and judicial rulings.[74] In essence UPICC "offer subsidiary rules when the domestic law is silent or unclear, or where it requires modernisation to be effectively applied in the international arena which is not its typical habitat."[75] Parties which are not confident in relying entirely on UPICC can simple declare the CISG as the governing law supplemented by UPICC.

The CEAC rules have the potential to be the neutral arbitral rules which will not only suit the civil but also the common law contract drafters. This is so as the rules allow the use of transnational laws specifically the CISG and most importantly UPICC. It is a compromise as it is not creating offence to the Chinese traders nor the EU or for that matter all the countries along the Silk Road. In essence the astute contract drafter will be able to choose the exact governing law as contained in article 35 CEAC which suits the circumstances and hence will make a contract more "user-friendly."

---

[74] For a full discussion see *Lake, S.*, An Empirical Study of the UNIDROIT Principles – International and British Responses, Unif. L. Rev. 2011 above n 41.
[75] Ibid at 694.

To What Extent Do the UNIDROIT Principles 2016 Restate International Commercial Law? Principles Familiar to Civil Law & Principles Unfamiliar to Common Law – a Continental European, in particular German Perspective –

Gerhard Wegen[*]
and Ref. jur. Benedikt Keil[**]

I. Introduction

The UNIDROIT Principles are a project of supra-regional contract law harmonisation. They primarily focus on the law of commercial contracts at the global level. The Principles are not based on specific national legal systems as models, nor do they essentially come from a single source, but form a joint work.[1]

There is already a 4th version, the UNIDROIT Principles ofInternational Commercial Contracts 2016, which in total include a preamble and 211 articles divided into 11 chapters (from *"General Provisions"* to *"Plurality of Obligors and Obligees"*).[2] The 4th version, however, do not cover all of the

---

[*] Prof. Dr. Gerhard Wegen, LL.M. (Harvard), Partner, GLEISS LUTZ, Stuttgart (Germany); admitted to the German (1981) and New York Bar (1983) and as Foreign Attorney in Brussels (1987); LL.M. Harvard Law School (1981); Dr. iur. Tübingen (1985); Professor at the Faculty of Law, University of Tübingen.

[**] Trainee lawyer, GLEISS LUTZ, Stuttgart (Germany).

[1] *Zimmermann*, Die Unidroit-Grundregeln der internationalen Handelsverträge 2004 in vergleichender Perspektive, ZEuP 2005, 264-290, 267.

[2] For detailed bibliographies of books and articles on the UNIDROIT Principles *see* *Brödermann* (ed.), Unidroit Principles of International Commercial Contracts, An Article-by-Article Commentary, 1st ed. (Hamburg) 2018, Bibliography (at p. L); *Vogenauer* (ed.), Commentary on the UNIDROIT Principles of International Commercial Contracts, 2nd ed. (Oxford) 2015, Appendix II (at p. 1402-1444 on a chapter-by-chapter-basis); www.unilex.info (at „UNIDROIT PRINCIPLES OF INTERNATIONAL CONTRACTS" and there „BIBLIOGRAPHY").

general contract law. For example, they explicitly waive a regulation on the lack of legal capacity (Art. 3.1.1)[3].

In the form of presentation, the UNIDROIT Principles are based on the US Restatements.[4] The text of the individual articles is followed by a commentary with application examples, whereby – in contrast to the Restatements – comparative legal notes are missing. The text of the comments refers only in part to the legal situation applicable in many, or most, states. It seems that the authors of the UNIDROIT Principles have had in mind above all the practical usefulness of their work for judges, arbitrators and merchants, for whom a handy book with concise explanations is more important than a scientific foundation. This can also be seen in the style in which the Principles are written. The style consciously strives for comprehensibility and tries to avoid legal jargon as far as possible, but the subsumability of the Principles is not inferior to that of the norms contained in the national codifications.

Driven by the question *"To what extent do the UNIDROIT Principles 2016 restate international commercial law?"* the authors of this essay examine the main familiarities to Civil Law, here focused on the example of Germany's Civil Code, and at the same time highlights the main unfamiliarities to Common Law. The appendix to this essay contains a tabular comparison.

II. Main Familiarities to Civil Law & Unfimiliarities to Common Law

1. General Provisions (chapter 1)

The UNIDROIT Principles are based on a few premises that are self-evident from a German point of view, such as[5]

---

3 Articles without designation are those of UNIDROIT Principles 2016.
4 *Zimmermann*, ZEuP 2005, 267.
5 For a list of the underlying general principles of the UNIDROIT Principles *see* *Brödermann*, Art. 1.7 no. 4, p. 30.

Art. 1.1	freedom of contract as a *„largely recognised around the globe although often only inherently"*[6] (Art. 2 para. 1 German Basic Law),
Art. 1.2	informality, *"a fundamental principle of international trade"*[7] and inspired *inter alia* by Art. 11 CISG (Art. 2 para. 1 German Basic Law),
Art. 1.3	binding character of a contract *"is common or inherent to most contract laws around the globe,[…] although the cultural understanding […] may vary[…]"*[8] (§ 241 para. 1 German Civil Code, *"pacta sunt servanda"*),
Art. 1.5	party autonomy (Art. 2 para. 1 German Basic Law),
Art. 1.7	good faith and fair dealing (*"Even if it is not enshrined around the globe in general and abstract legal rules […], most legal systems sanction actions in bad faith […] to the detriment of the contracting partner in one way or another […]. The wording of para. 1 reflects a compromise which englobes both the continental European legal systems' approach to subjective and objective aspects of good faith, and the common law's distinction between good faith and fair dealing […]."*[9]),
Art. 1.8	inconsistent behavior *"can be classified as a symbiosis of the venire contra factum proprium doctrine in civil [§ 242 German Civil Code] and the estoppel doctrine in common Law jurisdictions […] with due regard to similar principles in*

---

[6] *Brödermann*, Art 1.1 no. 1, p. 21; overview at Vogenauer/*Vogenauer*, Art. 1.1 no. 3.

[7] *Brödermann*, Art 1.2 no. 1, p. 22.

[8] *Brödermann*, Art. 1.3 no. 1, p. 23 with references, in notes 2 and 3, to Official Comments, Art. 1.3 no. 1, p. 9-10 and Morán Bovio (ed.)/*Viscasillas*, Commentaria a los Principios de UNIDROIT para los Contratos del Comercio Internacional, 2nd ed. (Pamplona) 2003, Art. 1.3 no. 1, p. 65; *see* e.g. Vogenauer/*Vogenauer*, Art 1.2 no. 3 with an analysis of the inherent importance of the principle within the CISG system.

[9] *Brödermann*, Art. 1.7 no. 1, p. 30-31 with reference, in notes 5 to 7, *inter alia* to Vogenauer/*Vogenauer*, Art. 1.7 no. 7 and (1992) Pil.-Misc. 18, p. 75 in combination with p- 62, 66, 69 and 74.

	transnational contexts, e.g. the lex mercatoria[...]"[10],
Art. 1.9	respect of usages and practices established between the parties and of general international trade usages as *"two widely recognised principles [...]"*[11] (§ 242 German Civil Code, § 346 German Commercial Code),
e.g. Art. 4.5	*"favour contractus"* principle, the policy to keep contracts alive whenever possible (§§ 139, 154, 155 German Civil Code),
Art. 5.1.3	duty of cooperation.

2. Contracting by Silence (chapter 2 section 1)

With regard to the question of how a contract can be concluded, the UNIDROIT Principles follow the same approaches as German law. Art. 2.1.1 covers firstly the classical offer and acceptance scenario (§§ 145 *et seq.* German Civil Code) and secondly the possibility of agreement by conduct which is a generally accepted principle in German law and in line with various other legal systems around the globe[12].

Like German law, the UNIDROIT Principles are based on the principle that simple silence is not an acceptance and is therefore of no legal significance (Art. 2.1.6(1) sent. 2). Under German law, however, silence can exceptionally also mean acceptance (or rejection). It then depends on legal rules (e.g.

---

[10] *Brödermann*, Art. 1.8 no. 1, p. 32 with reference, in notes 3-4, to *Bonell*, An International Restatement of Contract Law: The UNIDROIT Principles of International Commercial Law, 3[d] ed. (2005), p. 134 and Morán Bovio/*Melíndez*, Art. 1.8 no. 2.b, p. 90 and Vogenauer/*Vogenauer*, Art. 1.8 no. 1, 3.

[11] *Brödermann*, Art. 1.9 no. 1, p. 33 with reference, in note 7, to Arbitral Award 4 March 2004 (*ad hoc*), under 3., Unilex.info; and to Vogenauer/*Vogenauer*, Art. 1.8 no. 6-7, 11; *see* for the respect of general international usages the references in *Vogenauer*, Art. 1.9 no. 18.

[12] *Brödermann*, Art. 2.1.1 no. 2, p. 39, mentions in his footnote to no. 5 Art. 1120 French Civil Code (2016 version) (contract conclusion as an exception in case of silence); Vogenauer/*Nottage*, Art. 2.1.1 lists in his footnotes to no. 6 e.g. the laws of USA (§ 4 Restatement (Second) of Contracts; §§ 1-201(3) and (12), 2-204 UCC; also noted by Morán Bovio, Art. 2.1 no. 2.b, p. 110, Korea (Art. 532 Civil Code), Russia (Art. 432(1) Civil Code).

§ 516 para. 2 sent. 2 German Civil Code) or the will of the contracting parties whether silence is to be regarded as consent or rejection. In the context of commercial transactions between merchants, under German law silence is even of greater importance (e.g. § 362 para. 1 sent. 1, § 377 para. 2 German Commercial Code and the so-called *„Kaufmännisches Bestätigungsschreiben")*. The *"Kaufmännische Bestätigungsschreiben"* (*"commercial letter of confirmation"*), which is not explicitly regulated in the German Commercial Code but which is recognized as a commercial custom within the meaning of § 346 German Commercial Code, must be contradicted by a merchant without delay if he does not wish to accept the contents of this letter. If he does not react to a commercial letter of confirmation and remains silent, this may be interpreted as acceptance.[13]

The UNIDROIT Principles also provide for exceptions.[14] Silence does not amount to acceptance unless (i) established practices or usages between the parties (Art. 2.1.6(3), Art. 1.9(1)) may require otherwise, (ii) Art. 2.1.12 on *"writing in confirmation"* applies, or (iii) if the interpretation of the action of the offeror leads to a duty to speak, (iv) if, in case of contract for the sole benefit of the offeree, the circumstances and/or a specific Principle imply a duty to promptly speak up if acceptance is not wanted (example: silence upon an offer to release: Art. 5.1.9(2)).[15] Art. 2.1.12 goes less far than some European legal systems where the silence upon receipt of a commercial confirmation letter can serve also as evidence for the contract formation.[16] It contains a strange rule for many Common Law lawyers in that it permits, under certain circumstances, alterations of a contract by silence.[17]

---

[13] *Deckert*, Das kaufmännische und berufliche Bestätigungsschreiben, JuS 1998, p. 121 *et seq.*; *Lettl*, Das kaufmännische Bestätigungsschreiben, JuS 2008, p. 849 *et seq.*

[14] *Brödermann*, Art. 2.1.6 no. 4, p. 44.

[15] *Brödermann*, Art. 2.1.6 no. 4, p. 44 with references, in notes 12 to 18 *inter alia* to Morán Bovio/*Viscasillas,* Art. 2.6 no. 1, p. 127, Vogenauer/*Anderson* Art. 2.1.6 no. 14-17.

[16] *Brödermann*, Art. 1.1.12 no. 3, p. 51 with reference to Vogenauer/*Anderson,* Art. 2.1.12 no. 4.

[17] *Brödermann*, Art. 2.1.12 no. 3, p. 51 with references in note 16 to Vogenauer/*Anderson,* Art. 2.1.12 no.2.

3. Pre-Contractual Liability (chapter 2 section 1)

In regard of a broken deal Civil Law and Common Law systems have a fundamentally different understanding of negotiations. In Germany, for example, a party might walk away from a deal to a competing offeror by pricing in the *"reliance"* damage or *"negative"* interest, e.g. of attorney fees to be compensated to the other party after the initial deal breaks[18] (§ 280 para. 1 in conjunction with § 311 para. 2 in conjunction with § 241 para. 2 German Civil Code, *"culpa in contrahendo"*). Common Law systems usually do not have a pre-contractual liability until a contract is actually concluded. In England, for example, there is no general obligation of the parties to act to good faith.[19] Art. 2.1.15 provides a compromise by underlining the right not to agree in para. 1, but sanctioning breaking off negotiations in *"bad faith"* (paras. 2-3).

4. Contracting under Standard Terms (chapter 2 section 1)

In Arts. 2.1.19-2.1.22 the UNIDROIT Principles deal with the inclusion of standard terms in a contract, but not fully. Like German law, they establish a definition (Art. 2.1.19(2); § 305 para. 1 German Civil Code), determine the handling of surprising clauses (Art. 2.1.20; § 305c German Civil Code) and the conflict between standard terms and non-standard terms (Art. 2.1.21; § 305b German Civil Code) as well as the battle of forms (Art. 2.1.22; § 306 para. 2 German Civil Code[20]), but there are no Principles for abusive or unconscionable standard terms (§§ 307 *et seq.* German Civil Code) other than the general principles on good faith and fair dealing such as Art. 1.7 and Art. 7.1.6. In light of the fact that the content control of standard

---

[18] *Brödermann*, Art. 2.1.15 no. 1, p. 56.
[19] See *Brödermann*, Art. 2.1.15 no. 1, p. 55 footnote to no. 2.
[20] *Berger* in: Prütting/Wegen/Weinreich (eds.), BGB, 13th ed. (Köln) 2018 („PWW"), § 305 no. 41.

terms and conditions is not only a consumer protection measure but is primarily intended to correct a partial market failure, and that in Germany the case law on § 307 German Civil Code is dominated by cases from the area of commercial contracts, it is said, that there is a real need for regulation here.[21]

The UNIDROIT Principles are considered as more compatible for B2B-transactions than the consumer oriented German law.[22] The incorporation (Art. 2.1.19(1)) is less strict than German law (§ 305 para. 2, but also *see* § 310 para. 1 sent. 1 German Civil Code) but more restrictive than Italian and Dutch law.[23] But under the frame of the UNIDROIT Principles it is much easier to reach *"individual agreement"* (Art. 2.1.19(2)) as compared to German law (§ 305b German Civil Code).[24]

5. Authority of Agents (chapter 2 section 2)

The UNIDROIT Principles do not deal with the internal relationship between agent and principal (Art. 2.2.1(2); therefore, the title of chapter 2 section 2 is called *"authority of agents"*) and only relate to agency by contract (Art. 2.2.1(3); §§ 167-176 German Civil Code).

The UNIDROIT Principles regulate the establishment (Art. 2.2.2(1); § 167 German Civil Code) and the scope of the authority of the agent (Art. 2.2.2(2); §§ 133, 157 German Civil Code; § 50 German Commercial Code), the sub-agency (Art. 2.2.8; in German law the principal has to authorize the sub-agency), the liability of agent acting without or exceeding its authority (Art. 2.2.6; § 179 German Civil Code), the conflict of interests (Art. 2.2.7; § 181 German Civil Code), the ratification by the principal of a contract concluded by an agent without authority (Art. 2.2.9) with the possibility of a time limit for

---

[21] *Zimmermann*, ZEuP 2005, 287.

[22] *Brödermann*, Art. 2.1.19 no. 4, p. 63.

[23] *Bonell*, An International Restatement, p. 154-155, as cited by *Brödermann*, Art. 2.1.19 no. 3, p. 62, footnote to no. 19.

[24] *Brödermann*, Art. 2.1.19 no. 1, p. 62 with reference, in note 5, to Vogenauer/*Vogenauer,* Art. 1.4 no. 19; *Brödermann*, Hamburg Law Review 2016, p. 21, 26-29; Vogenauer/*Naudé*, Art. 2.1.19 no. 3.

ratification (Art. 2.2.9(2)) and the termination of authority (Art. 2.2.10).

The UNIDROIT Principles differentiate precisely between agency disclosed (Art. 2.2.3) and undisclosed (Art. 2.2.4). In German law, however, undisclosed agency (also called *"indirect representation"*, *"mittelbare Stellvertretung"*) is not regulated in the German Civil Code. The main case of *"mittelbare Stellvertretung"* is commission business under commercial law (§§ 383 *et seq.* German Commercial Code). According to the UNIDROIT Principles, in the case of disclosed agency for the establishment of direct legal relations between the third party and the principal, it is only important that an agent acts within the scope of his authority *"and the third party knew or ought to have known that the agent was acting as an agent"* (Art. 2.2.3(1)). In the case of undisclosed agency, i.e. when an agent acts within the scope of his authority but the third party neither knew nor ought to have known that the agent was acting as an agent (Art. 2.2.4(1)), only in the special case of Art. 2.2.4(2), when the represented party is a business and the agent represents itself to be the owner of that business, the third party may exercise also against the business the rights it has against the agent.

While the UNIDROIT Principles base a so-called *"Rechtsscheinsvollmacht"* on the general principle of good faith (Art. 1.7) and the prohibition of inconsistent behavior (Art. 1.8)[25] (with the consequence that the principal cannot invoke against the third party the lack of authority of the agent, Art. 2.2.5(2)), in German law the principles of *"Rechtsscheinsvollmacht"* (in particular *"Duldungs- und Anscheinsvollmacht"*) were developed from §§ 170 *et seq.* German Civil Code and § 56 German Commercial Code and have now become customary law.[26]

---

[25] Official Comments, Art. 2.2.5 no. 2, p. 84-85; *Brödermann*, Art. 2.2.5 no. 2, p. 71; Vogenauer/*Krebs*, Art. 2.2.5 no. 3.

[26] PWW/*Frensch*, § 167 no. 37.

6. Interpretation of Contracts, Statements and other Conduct (chapter 4)

There is an important difference between Civil Law and Common Law in the way in which contracts are interpreted.[27] While Common Law is primarily based on the wording, Civil Law focuses on the will of the contracting parties. Contracts under Common Law are often very detailed and extensive. One of the reasons for this is that the contract can only be relied upon if the relied upon rule is reflected in the actual wording of the contract. Therefore, an attempt is often made to anticipate all possible events and to expressly deal with them in the contract. Civil Law parties, on the other hand, will often consider it sufficient not to set out every aspect of the legal relationship in writing, as they expect the court to more accurately assess the intentions of the parties and the circumstances surrounding the conclusion of the contract in order to close any loopholes.

The UNIDROIT Principles provide a common ground merging these different approaches of interpretation, as evidenced by the observation of many scholars from different background that the UNIDROIT Principles *"provisions* [on interpretation], *or at least some of them, are essentially compatible"* with their respective domestic systems. Arts. 4.1 *et seq.* are inspired to a large extent by Art. 8 CISG (but go beyond it)[28] and to some extent by a comparative study of domestic laws.[29] The UNIDROIT Principles on interpretation have been describes as *"general principles of law"*[30] reflecting *"universal hermeneutic truths"* [31], the key rule in Art. 4.2(2) provides itself an application of the Principle of good faith and fair dealing (Art. 1.7).[32]

---

27 *Brödermann*, Art. 4.1 no. 1, p. 109.
28 *Brödermann*, Art. 4.1 no. 2, p. 110, footnote to no. 16: *"Art. 8 CISG relates solely to the interpretation of 'statements made by and other conduct of a party'."*
29 Vogenauer/*Vogenauer*, Introduction to chapter 4 of the PICC, no. 6 as cited by *Brödermann*, Art. 4.1 no. 2, p. 110.
30 Vogenauer/*Vogenauer*, Introduction to chapter 4 of the PICC, no. 8 as cited by *Brödermann*, Art. 4.1 no. 2, p. 110.
31 Vogenauer/*Vogenauer*, Introduction to chapter 4 of the PICC, no. 7 as cited by *Brödermann*, Art. 4.1 no. 2, p. 110.
32 *Bonell*, An Intrernational Restatement p. 142; Vogenauer/*Vogenauer*, Art. 4.3 no. 23, as both cited by *Brödermann*, Art. 4.1 no. 2, p. 110.

7. Release by Agreement (Art. 5.1.9)

Art. 5.1.9 stipulates that an obligee may release its right by agreement with the obligor. The UNIDROIT Principles thus lay down – as in § 397 German Civil Code (*"Erlassvertrag"*) – a contractual requirement. The UNIDROIT Principles and German law do not know of a unilateral waiver. Art. 5.1.9(2), however, foresees acceptance by fiction in the case of a free waiver if the obligor does not reject the waiver offer immediately after becoming aware of it.

8. Contracts in Favour of Third Parties (chapter 5 section 2)

In Arts. 5.2.1-5.2.6, the UNIDROIT Principles are based on a broad European consensus[33] on the subject of *"contract in favour of third party"*, when the third party (*"beneficiary"*) acquires his own right on the basis of the contract concluded between the promising party (*"promisor"*) and the recipient of the promise (*"promisee"*) (Art. 5.2.1(1)). The beneficiary does not need to agree. He can – consistent with § 333 German Civil Code – reject the right assigned to him (Art. 5.2.6); the right is then considered not to be acquired by him.

Art. 5.2.1(2) establishes as a general Principle – consistent with § 328 para. 2 German Civil Code – that *"the existence and the content of the beneficiary's right against the promisor are determined by the agreement of the parties and are subject to any conditions or other limitations under the agreement"*. Art. 5.2.5, however, allows the parties to modify or revoke the rights granted to the beneficiary until he has accepted them or has reasonably acted in reliance on them. This is consistent with a number of international instruments and national laws.[34]

---

[33] *Brödermann*, Art. 5.2.1 no. 1, p. 136 with reference to Vogenauer/*Vogenauer*, Art. 5.2.1 no. 6.

[34] Vogenauer/*Vogenauer*, Art. 5.2.5 no. 3 with reference to German law but also *inter alia* to Art. II.-9:303(2) DCFR, United Kingdom's 2(1) UK Contracts (Rights of Third Parties) Act 1999 and § 311(2) Restatement 2nd Contracts (USA); referenced by *Brödermann*, Art. 5.2.5 no. 1, p. 140.

According to § 334 German Civil Code, the promisor can assert against the third party all objections which the promisor could raise against the promisee (Art. 5.2.4).

9. Hardship (chapter 6 section 2)

With its roots in large international contracts, e.g. in some of the price *"adaption clauses"* or in *"economical clauses"*, and inspired by the possibility of adaption in case of a fundamental change of the basis of the contract in some Civil Law jurisdictions – such as § 313 German Civil Code – Arts. 6.2.1-6.2.3 transfer to all international contracts an innovative general (default) concept.[35] *"Hardship"* (aiming for performance like § 313 para. 1 German Civil Code) is distinct form *"force majeure"* (Art. 7.1.7(1), mainly concerned with non-performance), because performance is still (technically) possible under changed circumstances, although not at all any more on the basis of the initially intended and/or negotiated economic equilibrium of the parties.[36] *"Hardship"* primarily leads to renegotiation, whereby such renegotiation has to be requested without undue delay and with an indication of the grounds on which the request is based on (Art. 6.2.3(1)). The request for renegotiation, however, does not in itself entitle the disadvantaged party to withhold performance, but extreme circumstances underlying the notice may do so (Art. 1.7).[37] *"Upon failure to reach agreement within a reasonable time"* pursuant to Art. 6.2.3(3) the (allegedly) disadvantages party may apply to the court to either (i) terminate the contract whereby the court has discretion to determine the date and the terms or (ii) to adapt the contract with a view of restoring the equilibrium which may include *"a fair distribution of the losses"*[38] (which may, may not or may only partially be reflected in a price adaption). Courts may also decide in some circumstances to solve a certain

---

[35] Vogenauer/*McKendrick*, Introduction to Section 6.2 of the PICC, no. 10; *Brödermann*, Art. 6.2.1 no. 1, p. 176.
[36] *Brödermann*, Art. 6.2.1 no. 1, p. 177 with further references in notes 9-10.
[37] Official Comments, Art. 6.2.3 no. 4 and Illustration 4, p. 225; Vogenauer/*McKendrick*, Art. 6.2.3 no. 4 and Art. 7.4.1 no. 6 note 22; *Brödermann*, Art. 6.2.3 no. 2, p. 181.
[38] Official Comments, Art. 6.2.3 no. 7, p. 226.

impass between the parties and then trigger subsequent renegotiations by the parties themselves.[39]

According to § 313 para. 1 German Civil Code, the (allegedly) disadvantaged party can primarily demand adaption of the contract, as far as this is possible and reasonable, taking into account the interests of both sides. It is controversial whether a negotiation attempt is necessary before the judicial adjustment. While one opinion is in favour of the adjustment of the contract by the court[40], another opinion is in favour of the parties having to make their own efforts to adjust the contract first[41]. The latter view is favoured firstly by the wording ("*kann Anpassung verlangen*") and secondly by the intention of § 313 German Civil Code, which is to strengthen private autonomy by allowing contracts which are impaired by serious disruptions to be adapted by negotiation. This, however, requires that these adjustments remain in the hands of the parties for as long as possible and thus requires an attempt to negotiate the contract prior to a judicial act. If an adjustment of the contract is not possible or not reasonable for a part, the disadvantaged part can withdraw from the contract (§ 313 para. 3 sent. 1 German Civil Code). The right to withdraw from the contract shall be replaced by the right to terminate the contract in the case of continuous obligations (sent. 2).

10. Non-Performance (chapter 7)

According to the UNIDROIT Principles, non-performance is defined as the failure by a party to perform any of its obligations under the contract, including defective performance or delayed performance (Art. 7.1.1). Remedies are provided for these cases: (i) a right to cure non-performance for the obligor (Arts. 7.1.4-7.1.5), (ii) a right to terminate the contract (Arts. 7.3.1 *et seq.* and (iii) a right to damages (Arts. 7.4.1 *et seq.*). These remedies are similar to German law, but are by no means

---

[39] Official Comments, Art. 6.2.3 no. 7, p. 226; Vogenauer/*McKendrick*, Art. 6.2.3 no. 10; *Brödermann*, Art. 6.2.3 no. 3, p. 181.
[40] MünchKomm/*Roth*, BGB, Band no. 3, 7th ed. (Munich) 2017, § 313 no. 93.
[41] PWW/*Stürner*, § 313 no. 20 *et seq.*

integrated into such a differentiated system as in German law (§§ 280 *et seq.*, 323 *et seq.*, 346 *et seq.*, in conjunction with e.g. § 437 or § 634 German Civil Code).

If the UNIDROIT Principles are applied, the buyer can only reduce the purchase price if a reduction right has been contractually agreed, while according to German law (§ 441 German Civil Code) the buyer is entitled to a right of reduction by law. This shows the influence of Common Law on the UNIDROIT Principles; this remedy is also not recognized there.[42]

Arts. 7.1.4-7.1.5 grants the non-performing party the right to cure the non-performance. This right is not precluded by a notice of termination (Art. 7.1.4(2)), whereas according to German law *"Rücktritt"* and *"Nacherfüllung"* are mutually exclusive. But if the cure of the non-performance is effectively notified, the rights of the aggrieved party that are inconsistent with the non-performing party's performance are suspended until the time for cure has expired (Art. 7.1.4(3)). Notwithstanding cure, the aggrieved party retains the right to claim damages for delay as well as for any harm caused or not prevented by the cure (Art. 7.1.4(5); § 325 German Civil Code).

The right to terminate the contract is governed by chapter 7 section 3 (§§ 323 *et seq.*, 346 *et seq.* German Civil Code). A party may terminate the contract by notice of termination (Art. 7.3.2(1); § 349 German Civil Code) either (i) if the non-performance of an obligation under the contract by the other party amounts a fundamental non-performance (Art. 7.3.1(1); § 324 German Civil Code) or (ii) in case of delay, if the other party fails to perform before the expiration of the time limit allowed it under Article 7.1.5 (Article 7.3.1(3); § 323 para. 1 alt. 1 German Civil Code). Where prior to the date for performance by one of the parties it is clear that there will be a fundamental non-performance by that party, the other party may terminate the contract (Art. 7.3.3; § 323 para. 4 German Civil Code). The right to termination, however, is tempered – in line with an

---

[42] *Zimmermann*, ZEuP 2005, 272.

international trend[43] and the general *"favour contractus"* approach – by four restrictions[44]: (i) a threshold provided by the factors in para. 2, (ii) the *"Nachfrist-"*mechanism pursuant to Art. 7.1.5 in case of delay (para. 3), which requires granting additional time (in German: *"Nachfrist"*; § 323 para. 1 German Civil Code) prior to a termination for delay, (iii) the right to cure of the non-performing party (Art. 7.1.4) and finally (iv) by the behaviour of the obligee itself who cannot change back to (full) termination after accepting a price reduction[45]. The termination does not preclude claims for damages due to non-performance (Art. 7.3.5(2); § 325 German Civil Code). The UNIDROIT Principles make an explicit distinction between contracts to be performed at one time (Art. 7.3.6) and long-term contracts (Art. 7.3.7). In the latter case, return may only be claimed for the period after the termination has taken effect, provided that the contract is divisible.

A claim for damages (aimed at full compensation, Art. 7.4.2(1)) exists according to Art. 7.4.1(1) either exclusively or in conjunction with any other remedies (§ 325 German Civil Code), except where the non-performance is excused under these Principles. The claim may also be directed to non-pecuniary damage which includes, for instance, physical suffering and emotional distress (Art. 7.4.2(2); § 253 German Civil Code). The UNIDROIT Principles also regulate the case where the damage was partially caused by the aggrieved party (Art. 7.4.7; § 254 para. 1 German Civil Code) or could have been reduced by that party (Art. 7.4.8; § 254 para. 2 German Civil Code).

11. Set-Off (chapter 8)

In general, the UNIDROIT Principles follow the German model of set-off by declaration (Art. 8.3; § 388 German Civil Code). The requirements for set-off are basically the same: mutuality, liabilities of the same type, due date of the counterclaim and

---

[43] Vogenauer/*Huber*, Introduction to Section 7.3. of the UNIDROIT Principles, no. 7 (praising the termination concet of the UNIDROIT Principles as a *"model"*).
[44] *Brödermann*, Art. 7.3.1 no. 1, p. 218.
[45] *Brödermann*, Art. 7.2.5 no. 1, p. 218.

fulfillability of the principal claim (Art. 8.1; § 387 German Civil Code). In addition, the UNIDROIT Principles also have a fifth requirement, based on the French model: the liquidity of the counterclaim (Art. 8.1(1)(b): „[...] *the other party's obligation is ascertained as to its existence and amount* [...]").[46] However, the situation in which the obligations of both parties are based on the same legal relationship is privileged (Art. 8.1(2)), since this legal relationship must be clarified by the judge dealing with the passive claim anyway.

The fact that the parties owe each other money in different currencies does not prevent set-off, unless they have agreed that the set-off party only has to pay in a certain currency (Art. 8.2). Art. 8.2 also requires that both currencies are freely convertible.

In contrast to German law, however, no retroactive effect (*"ex tunc"*) is attributed to the set-off declaration (Art. 8.5(3); § 389 German Civil Code). In addition, UNIDROIT Principles lack regulations on the exclusion of the right of set-off corresponding to §§ 392-395 of the German Civil Code.

12. Assignment of Rights (chapter 9 section 1)

Like German law, according to UNIDROIT Principles a right can be transferred informally by agreement between the assignor and the assignee (Art. 9.1.7(1); § 398 sent. 1 German Civil Code). The UNIDROIT Principles also permit the assignment of future rights (Art. 9.1.5) and the assignment in bundles (Art. 9.1.6).

It seems, that the UNIDROIT Principles pursue a decidedly more assignment friendly approach than German law. For example, the assignment may be effective despite the contractual prohibition, but the assignor may be liable to the obligor for breach of contract (Art. 9.1.9; § 399 alt. 2 in conjunction with § 134 German Civil Code). But an exception of

---

[46] *Zimmermann*, ZEuP 2005, 280.

the *"pactum de non cedendo"* principle is provided by § 354a German Commercial Code in case of money demands, if the obligor and the assignor are merchants. If an assignment takes place despite the agreed prohibition, the assignment is nevertheless effective. But the obligor can alternatively discharge his obligation of the assignor (§ 354a para. 1 sent. 2 German Commercial Code).

With regard to the question of discharge (Art. 9.1.10) and questions of priority in the case of multiple assignments (Art. 9.1.11), the UNIDROIT Principles explicitly refer to notification to the obligor, whereas German law refers to the positive knowledge of the obligor (§§ 406, 407, 408 German Civil Code). Similarities do exist in regards of the protection of the obligor: (i) under which circumstances the obligor retains a right of set-off against the new assignee (Art. 9.1.13; § 406 German Civil Code), (ii) to what extent the assignor and the obligor may still modify the assigned right with effect for and against the assignee and (iii) when will the obligor be released by payment to the previous or new assignee (Arts. 9.1.10 *et seq.*; § 407 German Civil Code). Essentially identical to German law, the UNIDROIT Principles stipulate that the obligor may assert against the assignee all defences that the obligor could assert against the assignor (Art. 9.1.13(1); § 404 German Civil Code). Art. 9.1.14 contains – as in German law (§ 401 BGB) – a regulation on the transfer of rights relating to the assigned right (in particular rights to secure performance).

13. Transfer of Obligations (chapter 9 section 2)

As a counterpart to the assignment of rights, the Arts. 9.2 *et seq.* regulates the transfer of obligations. The UNIDROIT Principles cover not only the privative (discharging) transfer of obligations (Art. 9.2.5(1); §§ 414 *et seq.* German Civil Code), but also a kind of cumulative assumption of obligation (Art. 9.2.5(3); § 311 para. 1 German Civil Code) as well as the assumption of an obligation to perform (Art. 9.2.6; § 329 German Civil Code *"Erfüllungsübernahme"*).

The mechanism of debt assumption is the same as in German law: An assumption of an obligation is either concluded by an agreement between the original obligor and the new obligor, whereby the obligee must agree to this debt assumption agreement (Art. 9.2.1(a), Art. 9.2.3; § 415 German Civil Code), or by an agreement between the obligee and the new obligor, whereby the new obligor assumes the obligation (Art. 9.2.1(b); § 414 German Civil Code). In the latter case, the UNIDROIT Principles waive the consent of the previous obligor.

The effects of the transfer of obligations on defences (Art. 9.2.7(1); § 417 para. 1 sent. 1), the rights of set-off (Art. 9.2.7(2); § 417 para. 1 sent. 2) and securities (Art. 9.2.8; § 418 para. 1 German Civil Code) are uniform.

14. Assignment of Contracts (chapter 9 section 3)

In Arts. 9.3.1-Art. 9.3.7, the UNIDROIT Principles deal with the assignment of contracts. In German law, this corresponds to the contractual transfer of a contract, which is understood as a *"sui generis"* contract (§ 311 para. 1 German Civil Code).[47] The UNIDROIT Principles are also based on the principle that the third party affected by the contract must also agree to the transaction (Art. 9.3.3).

Basically, the Principles of the assignment of contracts are modelled on those of the previous sections (assignment of rights, transfer of obligations). In addition to the privative (Art. 9.3.5(1)), a kind of cumulative contract transfer (Art. 9.3.5(3)) is also recognized.

15. Limitations Periods (chapter 10)

Chapter 10 of the UNIDROIT Principles is entitled *"Limitation Periods"*. This heading sets the UNIDROIT Principles apart from the purely procedural understanding of a Common Law lawyer.

---

[47] PWW/*Müller*, § 398 no. 27.

Instead, he speaks of *"limitation of actions"* which does not affect the right as such (the *"cause of action"*) and which tends to affect the possibility of pursuing this right in court.[48] The UNIDROIT Principles, on the other hand, understand the statute of limitations – like the German legal system – as an institute of substantive law (Art. 10.9; § 214 German Civil Code). At the end of the limitation period, the right concerned does not cease to exist, the obligor is only entitled to refuse performance.[49] However, the title of the chapter (*"Limitation Periods"*) is inaccurate insofar as it deals not only with limitation periods but also with the structure of the limitation regime.

The UNIDROIT Principles stipulate a general limitation period of three years (Art. 10.2(1); § 195 German Civil Code) and also stipulate a maximum limitation period of ten years (Art. 10.2(2); § 199 para. 3 no. 1 German Civil Code), which – as in German law – runs alongside the general limitation period. One difference, however, is that the UNIDROIT Principles provide for a uniform maximum period of ten years, while German law differentiates: thirty years for claims based on the infringement of personal rights (or for inheritance claims), otherwise ten years (§ 199 para. 2-3a German Civil Code). This can be explained by the fact that Chapter 10 of the UNIDROIT Principles only refers to the exercise of rights *"governed by the Principles"* (Art. 10.1(1)), i.e. contractual rights.[50] However, the legal principle of limitation periods remains the same: On the one hand legal certainty for the obligor, on the other hand the obligee must be given a fair chance to pursue his rights. Therefore, a short, knowledge-dependent general limitation period is combined with a longer, knowledge-independent maximum period.

The beginning of the run of the general limitation period is, according to Art. 10.2 (somewhat complicated[51]), *"the day after the day the obligee knows or ought to have known the facts as a result of which the obligee's right can be exercised"*, whereas under German law the general limitation period begins at the

---

[48] *Zimmermann*, ZEuP 2005, 271; *Birks*, Englisch Private Law, 2000.
[49] *Zimmermann*, JZ 2000, 853, 856 *et seq.*
[50] *Zimmermann*, ZEuP 2005, 272.
[51] *Zimmermann*, ZEuP 2005, 273.

end of the year in which (i) the claim arose and (ii) the obligee becomes aware of the circumstances giving rise to the claim and of the obligor's person or ought to be aware of them without gross negligence (§ 199 para. 1 German Civil Code). Both the UNIDROIT Principles and German law thus provide for a recognisability criterion in their system of limitation law and place the burden of proof on the obligor. However, as already mentioned[52], the UNIDROIT Principles do not contain an explicit regulation on the beginning of the limitation period for non-contractual claims for damages or omission.

The parties may contractually shorten and extend the limitation periods, but not to less than one year and not to more than fifteen years (Art. 10.3; § 202 German Civil Code).

The initiation of judicial proceedings (Art. 10.5(1)(a); § 204 para. 1 no. 1 German Civil Code), insolvency proceedings (Art. 10.5(1)(b); § 204 para. 1 no. 10 German Civil Code) and, if the obligor is a dissolving legal entity, dissolution proceedings (Art. 10.5(1)(c)) merely suspend the beginning of the limitation period and do not lead to an interruption of the limitation period. The same applies in the case of arbitration proceedings (Art. 10.6; § 204 para. 1 no. 11 German Civil Code) or in the case of alternative dispute resolution proceedings (Art. 10.7; § 204 para. 1 no. 4 German Civil Code). *"Force majeure"* also constitutes a ground for suspension (Art. 10.8(1); § 206 German Civil Code). While Art. 10.8(2) lists the lack of legal capacity and death as two further reasons for suspension, German law provides for a so-called *"Ablaufhemmung"*, delaying the expiration of a limitation period under certain conditions (§§ 210, 211 German Civil Code). In the case of an acknowledgement, however, the general limitation period begins to run again as in German law (Art. 10.4; § 212 para. 1 no. 1 German Civil Code). In contrast to German law, however, there is no regulation according to which negotiations between the parties of the claim or of the circumstances from which a claim may arise hinder the expiry of the limitation period. German law provides a separate rule for this (§ 203 German Civil Code). Most other legal systems also take this regulatory concept into account in some way or

---

[52] *See* footnote no. 42.

another.[53] The authors of the UNIDROIT Principles, on the other hand, point the parties to the possibility of an explicit agreement extending the statute of limitations and thus underline the specific aim of the UNIDROIT Principles in relation to international trade agreements.

According to Art. 10.9(3), a right can still be relied on as a defence, even if the expiration of the limitation period for that right has been asserted. Defences fall under this Principle, in particular the right of retention under Art. 8.1.3. The obligee's right of set-off, on the other hand, is made dependent in Art. 10.10 on the obligor's plea of limitation being raised. Thereafter, set-off is no longer possible if the obligor has raised the plea of limitation. German law, on the other hand, in the case of set-off and right of retention, focuses solely on whether the claim was not statute-barred at the time at which it was first possible to set off or refuse performance (§ 215 German Civil Code).

What has been paid to fulfil a claim – again in accordance with German law – cannot be reclaimed simply because the limitation period has expired (Art. 10.11; § 214 para. 1 sent. 1 German Civil Code).

A (further) important difference to German law is that the limitation period under Art. 10.1 refers to contractual claims[54]; this is meant when it states the exercise of rights *" governed by the principles"*. In contrast, the German limitation rules cover both contractual and non-contractual claims (§ 194 German Civil Code). However, the scope of Art. 10.1 proves to be wider in that the statute of limitations also applies to the exercise of rights *"which directly affect the contract"*, as the official commentary no. 1 para. 1 on Art. 10.1 says.[55] The contractually agreed right to terminate the contract and a reduction right are cited as examples. According to the German understanding, these are rights which alter the legal relationship

---

[53] *Zimmermann*, ZEuP 2005, 277; *Zimmermann/Whittaker* (ed.), Good Faith in European Contract Law, 2000, p. 493 *et seq.*
[54] *See* footnote no. 42.
[55] Official Comments, Art. 10.1 no. 1, p. 349: „*but also the exercise of rights which directly affect a contract, such as the right of termination or a right of price reduction contractually agreed upon.*".

(*"Gestaltungsrechte"*). However, it is questionable whether such a regulation makes sense, in particular because a more specific exclusion period applies to the right to terminate the contract anyway (Art. 7.3.2(1)).[56]

The UNIDROIT Principles – in contrast to most national laws – do not contain any regulation on the limitation of claims awarded by judgement[57] and claims to interest and other ancillary benefits[58]. Although the authors of the commentary on Art. 10.2 deal with the limitation of ancillary claims, they do not say why they consider a special rule unnecessary.[59] In light of the regulatory purpose of such a regulation a special rule appears necessary, because the concern pursued by the statute of limitation would be undermined if the obligee could still sue the obligor for the payment of interest accrued in respect of the main claim which is statute-barred, and the obligor could then be forced to address the merits of the main claim himself in order to defend himself.[60] The UNIDROIT Principles also do not contain any regulations on the restart of the limitation period in the event of an enforcement attempt (§ 212 para. 1 no. 2 German Civil Code). This is probably due to the fact that they also do not know any particular limitation period for a claim awarded by judgment.

16. Plurality of Obligors and of Obligees (chapter 11)

Chapter 11 of the UNIDROIT Principles deals with the plurality of obligors and obligees. *"Separate obligations"* (Art. 11.1.1(b)) and *"joint and several obligations"* (Art. 11.1.1(a); § 421 German Civil Code) as well as the respective counterparts *"separate claims"* (Art. 11.2.1(a)) and *"joint and several claims"* (Art.

---

[56] *Zimmermann*, ZEuP 2005, 272.
[57] *Zimmermann*, ZEuP 2005, 275, footnote to no. 77 is referring to § 197 para. 1 no. 3 German Civil Code, Art. 268 Astikos Kodikas, Art. 311 para. 1 Portuguese Código Civil, Art. 3:234 BW.
[58] *Zimmermann*, ZEuP 2005, 275, footnote to no. 80 is referring to § 217 German Civil Code, Art. 274 Astikos Kodikas, Art. 27 UNCITRAL Limitation Convention, Art. 3:312 BG.
[59] Official Comments, Art. 10.2 no. 10, p. 355.
[60] *Zimmermann*, ZEuP 2005, 276.

11.2.1(b); § 428 German Civil Code) are taken into account. As in German law, *"joint claims" (*Art. 11.2.1(c); §§ 432, 741 *et seq.* German Civil Code and the so-called *"Gesamthandsgemeinschaften"*) are also taken into account as the third type of plurality of obligees, whereas there is no explicit regulation on the *"joint obligations" ("Schuldnergemeinschaft"*).

III. Conclusion

The observations above have shown that the UNIDROIT Principles have much in common with German law. To answer to the question *"To what extent do the UNIDROIT Principles restate international commercial law?"* it can be said, that they represent a distillation of all relevant and important rules of German law relating to international trade contracts, whereby the authors of the UNIDROIT Principles attempted to make them more comprehensible.

Annex:

Tabular Comparison
UNIDROIT Principles 2016 – Civil Law – Common Law

ANNEX: TABULAR COMPARISON[61]

UNIDROIT Principles 2016	Civil Law	Common Law
PREAMBLE (Purpose of the Principles)		
CHAPTER 1: GENERAL PROVISIONS		
Article 1.1 (Freedom of contract)	➔ **Art. 2 para. 1 German Basic Law** ➔ **Art. 1102(1) French Civil Code**	
Article 1.2 (No form required)	➔ **Art. 2 para. 1 German Basic Law**	
Article 1.3 (Binding character of contract)	➔ **§ 241 para. 1 German Civil Code** (*"pacta sunt servanda"*) ➔ **Art. 1103(1) French Civil Code** (*"le contrat est la loi des parties"*)	
Article 1.4 (Mandatory rules)		
Article 1.5 (Exclusion or modification by the parties)		
Article 1.6 (Interpretation and supplementation of the Principles)		
Article 1.7 (Good faith and fair dealing)	➔ **§ 242 German Civil Code** (*"Treu und Glauben"*) ➔ **Art. 1104 French Civil Code** ➔ **Art. 6 and 60(2) Contract Law of the People's Republic of China** ➔ **Art. 1061 Códico Civil y Comercial Argentine** ➔ **Art. 1375 Québec Civil Code**	➔ **§ 205 Restatement 2nd Contracts (USA)** ➔ **Arts. 12, 39 Israelian Contracts (General Part) Law, 1973**
Article 1.8 (Inconsistent behaviour)	➔ **§ 242 German Civil Code** (*"venire contra factum proprium"*; *"Verwirkung"*)	*"estoppel"* doctrine

---

61   Based on *Vogenauer* (ed.), Commentary on the UNIDROIT Principles of International Commercial Contracts, 2nd ed. (Oxford) 2015, and, especially for references to French law, *Brödermann* (ed.), Unidroit Principles of International Commercial Contracts, An Article-by-Article Commentary, (Baden-Baden) 2018.

UNIDROIT Principles 2016	Civil Law	Common Law
Article 1.9 (Usages and practices)	➔ **§ 242 German Civil Code, § 346 German Commercial Code**	
Article 1.10 (Notice) **Article 1.11** (Definitions) **Article 1.12** (Computation of time set by parties)		

CHAPTER 2: FORMATION AND AUTHORITY OF AGENTS

Section 1: Formation

Article 2.1.1 (Manner of formation)	➔ **§§ 145-157 German Civil Code** ➔ **Art. 1120 French Civil Code** (contract conclusion as an exception in case of silence) ➔ **Art. 532 Korean Civil Code** ➔ **Art. 432(1) Russian Civil Code**	➔ **§ 4 Restatement 2nd Contracts (USA)** ➔ **§§ 1-201(3) and (12), 2-204 UCC**
Article 2.1.2 (Definition of offer)	➔ *"invitation ad offerendum"*	
Article 2.1.3 (Withdrawal of offer)		
Article 2.1.4 (Revocation of offer)	➔ **§ 130 German Civil Code**	➔ **§ 42 Restatement 2nd Contracts (USA)** ➔ **§ 2-205 UCC**
Article 2.1.5 (Rejection of offer)	➔ **§ 146 German Civil Code**	
Article 2.1.6 (Mode of acceptance)		
Article 2.1.7 (Time of acceptance)	➔ **§ 147 German Civil Code**	
Article 2.1.8 (Acceptance within a fixed period of time)	➔ **§ 148 German Civil Code**	
Article 2.1.9 (Late acceptance. Delay in transmission)	➔ **§ 149 German Civil Code**	
Article 2.1.10 (Withdrawal of acceptance)	➔ **§ 130 German Civil Code**	
Article 2.1.11 (Modified acceptance)	➔ **§ 150 German Civil Code**	
Article 2.1.12 (Writings in confirmation)	➔ *"Kaufmännisches Bestätigungsschreiben"*	

UNIDROIT Principles 2016	Civil Law	Common Law
Article 2.1.13 (Conclusion of contract dependent on agreement on specific matters or in a particular form)	➔ **§ 158 German Civil Code**	
Article 2.1.14 (Contract with terms deliberately left open)	➔ **§§ 154, 315 para. 3, 317 German Civil Code** ➔ **Art. 2 Swiss Code of Obligations** ➔ **Art. 1387 Civil Code of Québec**	➔ **§ 2-204(3) UCC**
Article 2.1.15 (Negotiations in bad faith)	➔ **§§ 280 para 1, 311 para. 2, 241 para. 2 German Civil Code** (*"culpa in contrahendo"*)	
Article 2.1.16 (Duty of confidentiality)		*"equitable wrong"*
Article 2.1.17 (Merger clauses)		
Article 2.1.18 (Modification in a particular form)	➔ *"einfache Schriftformklausel", „doppelte Schriftformklausel"*	
Article 2.1.19 (Contracting under standard terms)	➔ **§§ 305 *et seq.* German Civil Code**)	
Article 2.1.20 (Surprising terms)	➔ **§ 305c German Civil Code**	
Article 2.1.21 (Conflict between standard terms and non-standard terms)	➔ **§ 305b German Civil Code** ➔ **Art. 1342 Italian Civil Code**	➔ **§ 203(d) Restatement 2nd Contracts (USA)**
Article 2.1.22 (Battle of forms)	➔ **§ 306 para. 2 German Civil Code:** *"total knock out"* doctrine (where none of the standard terms apply) ➔ **Dutch *"first shot"* doctrine**	➔ **Common Law *"last shot"* doctrine** (where the terms sent out last may prevail)

Section 2: Authority of agents

Article 2.2.1 (Scope of the Section	➔ **§§ 167-176 German Civil Code**	
Article 2.2.2 (Establishment and scope of the authority of the agent)	➔ **§§ 167, 133, 157 German Civil Code, § 50 German Commercial Code**	
Article 2.2.3 (Agency disclosed)	➔ **§ 164 para. 1 German Civil Code**	
Article 2.2.4 (Agency undisclosed)	➔ **§§ 383 *et seq.* German Commercial Code**	
Article 2.2.5 (Agent	➔ **§§ 170 *et seq.* German Civil**	

UNIDROIT Principles 2016	Civil Law	Common Law
acting without or exceeding its authority) **Article 2.2.6** (Liability of agent acting without or exceeding its authority)	**Code** (*"Anscheins- / Duldungsvollmacht"*) ➔ **§ 179 German Civil Code**	
Article 2.2.7 (Conflict of interests)	➔ **§ 181 German Civil Code**	
Article 2.2.8 (Sub-agency)	➔ under **German law** the principal has to authorize the sub-agency	
Article 2.2.9 (Ratification)		
Article 2.2.10 (Termination of authority)	➔ **§§ 677-687 German Civil Code** (*„negotiorum gestio" / „gestion d'affaires" / "Geschäftsführung ohne Auftrag"*)	

CHAPTER 3: VALIDITY

Section 1: General Provisions

Article 3.1.1 (Matters not covered)	➔ **§§ 1, 2, 104** *et seq.* **German Civil Code**	
Article 3.1.2 (Validity of mere agreement)	➔ **§§ 145** *et seq.* **German Civil Code** requires a real contract without handing over of a good (*"Trennungsprinzip", "Abstraktionsprinzip"*). ➔ **Art. 1108 Belgian Civil Code** requires a cause. ➔ **Art. 1128 French Civil Code** does not require a cause anymore.	
Article 3.1.3 (Initial impossibility)	➔ **§ 311a para. 1 German Civil Code** does not lead to the invalidity of the contract. ➔ **Arts. 1163(2), 1178(1) 1st sentence French Civil Code** leads to the invalidity of the contract.	
Article 3.1.4 (Mandatory character of the provisions)		

Section 2: Grounds for

UNIDROIT Principles 2016	Civil Law	Common Law

avoidance

Article 3.2.1 (Definition of mistake)		
Article 3.2.2 (Relevant mistake)	➜ **§§ 119, 120, 123 German Civil Code**	
Article 3.2.3 (Error in expression or transmission)	➜ **§§ 119 para. 1 alt. 2, 120 German Civil Code**	
Article 3.2.4 (Remedies for non-performance)	➜ **§§ 437, 634 German Civil Code**	
Article 3.2.5 (Fraud)	➜ **§ 123 para. 1 alt. 1 German Civil Code**	
Article 3.2.6 (Threat)	➜ **§ 123 para. 1 alt. 2 German Civil Code**	
Article 3.2.7 (Gross disparity)	➜ **§ 138 German Civil Code**	
Article 3.2.8 (Third persons)	➜ **§ 123 para. 2 German Civil Code**	
Article 3.2.9 (Confirmation)	➜ **§ 144 German Civil Code**	
Article 3.2.10 (Loss of right to avoid)		
Article 3.2.11 (Notice of avoidance)	➜ **§ 143 German Civil Code** ➜ **Art. 1178(2) sent. 2 of the French Civil Code** requires the decision of a court (with an exception in case of party agreement)	
Article 3.2.12 (Time limits)	➜ **§§ 121, 124 German Civil Code**	➜ **§ 381(3) Restatement 2nd Contracts (USA)**
Article 3.2.13 (Partial avoidance)	➜ **§ 139 German Civil Code**	
Article 3.2.14 (Retroactive effect of avoidance)	➜ **§ 142 para. 1 German Civil Code**	
Article 3.2.15 (Restitution)	➜ **§ 812 para. 1 sent. 1 alt. 1 German Civil Code**	
Article 3.2.16 (Damages)	➜ **§ 122 German Civil Code**	
Article 3.2.17 (Unilateral declarations)		

Section 3: Illegality

Article 3.3.1 (Contracts infringing mandatory rules)	➜ **§ 134 German Civil Code**	
Article 3.3.2	➜ **§ 812 para. 1 sent. 1 alt. 1**	

UNIDROIT Principles 2016	Civil Law	Common Law
(Restitution)	**German Civil Code**	

CHAPTER 4: INTERPRETATION

Article 4.1 (Intention of the parties)	➔ **§§ 133, 157 German Civil Code**	
Article 4.2 (Interpretation of statements and other conduct)	➔ **§§ 133, 157 German Civil Code**	
Article 4.3 (Relevant circumstances)		
Article 4.4 (Reference to contract or statement as a whole)		
Article 4.5 (All terms to be given effect)		
Article 4.6 (Contra proferentem rule)	➔ **§ 305c para. 2 German Civil Code**	
Article 4.7 (Linguistic discrepancies)		
Article 4.8 (Supplying an omitted term)	➔ *"ergänzende Vertragsauslegung"*	➔ **§ 204 Restatement 2nd Contracts (USA)**

CHAPTER 5: CONTENT, THIRD PARTY RIGHTS AND CONDITIONS

Section 1: Content

Article 5.1.1 (Express and implied obligations)		
Article 5.1.2 (Implied obligations)		
Article 5.1.3 (Co-operation between the parties)		
Article 5.1.4 (Duty to achieve a specific result. Duty of best efforts)		
Article 5.1.5 (Determination of kind of duty involved)		
Article 5.1.6 (Determination of quality of performance)		
Article 5.1.7 (Price determination)		
Article 5.1.8 (Termination of a	➔ *e.g. §§ 573 et seq., 608, 620 et seq.* **German Civil Code**	

UNIDROIT Principles 2016	Civil Law	Common Law

contract for an indefinite period)
Article 5.1.9 (Release by agreement) | ➜ **§ 397 German Civil Code** |

Section 2: Third party rights

Article 5.2.1 (Contracts in favour of third parties) | ➜ **§ 328 German Civil Code** |
Article 5.2.2 (Third party identifiable) | |
Article 5.2.3 (Exclusion and limitation clauses) | |
Article 5.2.4 (Defences) | ➜ **§ 334 German Civil Code** |
Article 5.2.5 (Revocation) | ➜ **§ 328 para. 2 German Civil Code** | ➜ **§ 311(2) Restatement 2nd Contracts (USA)** |
Article 5.2.6 (Renunciation) | ➜ **§ 333 German Civil Code** |

Section 3: Conditions

Article 5.3.1 (Types of condition) | ➜ **§ 158 German Civil Code** |
Article 5.3.2 (Effect of conditions) | ➜ **§ 158 German Civil Code** |
Article 5.3.3 (Interference with conditions) | ➜ **§ 162 German Civil Code** |
Article 5.3.4 (Duty to preserve rights) | ➜ **§§ 160, 161 German Civil Code** |
Article 5.3.5 (Restitution in case of fulfilment of a resolutive condition) | ➜ **§§ 812 *et seq.* German Civil Code** |

CHAPTER 6: PERFORMANCE

Section 1: Performance in General

Article 6.1.1 (Time of performance) | ➜ **§ 271 German Civil Code** |
Article 6.1.2 (Performance at one time or in instalments) | |

UNIDROIT Principles 2016	Civil Law	Common Law
Article 6.1.3 (Partial performance)	➔ **§ 266 German Civil Code**	
Article 6.1.4 (Order of performance)		
Article 6.1.5 (Earlier performance)		
Article 6.1.6 (Place of performance)	➔ **§ 269 German Civil Code**	
Article 6.1.7 (Payment by cheque or other instrument)		
Article 6.1.8 (Payment by funds transfer)		
Article 6.1.9 (Currency of payment)		
Article 6.1.10 (Currency not expressed)		
Article 6.1.11 (Costs of performance)		
Article 6.1.12 (Imputation of payments)		
Article 6.1.13 (Imputation of non-monetary obligations)		
Article 6.1.14 (Application for public permission)		
Article 6.1.15 (Procedure in applying for permission)		
Article 6.1.16 (Permission neither granted nor refused)		
Article 6.1.17 (Permission refused)		

Section 2: Hardship

Article 6.2.1 (Contract to be observed)		
Article 6.2.2 (Definition of hardship)	➔ **§ 313 German Civil Code**	
Article 6.2.3 (Effects of hardship)	➔ **§ 313 para. 1 and 3 German Civil Code**	

CHAPTER 7: NON-

UNIDROIT Principles 2016	Civil Law	Common Law

PERFORMANCE

Section 1: Non-performance in general

Article 7.1.1 (Non-performance defined)
Article 7.1.2 (Interference by the other party)

Article 7.1.3 (Withholding performance)	➔ **§ 273 German Civil Code**

Article 7.1.4 (Cure by non-performing party)

Article 7.1.5 (Additional period for performance)	➔ **§ 323 para. 1 alt. 1 German Civil Code**

Article 7.1.6 (Exemption clauses)
Article 7.1.7 (Force majeure)

Section 2: Right to performance

Article 7.2.1 (Performance of monetary obligation)
Article 7.2.2 (Performance of non-monetary obligation)

Article 7.2.3 (Repair and replacement of defective performance)	➔ **§§ 434 *et seq.* German Civil Code**

Article 7.2.4 (Judicial penalty)
Article 7.2.5 (Change of remedy)

Section 3: Termination

Article 7.3.1 (Right to terminate the contract)	**§§ 323 *et seq.*, 346 *et seq.* German Civil Code**
Article 7.3.2 (Notice of termination)	**§ 349 German Civil Code**
Article 7.3.3 (Anticipatory non-	**§ 323 para. 4 German Civil Code**

69

UNIDROIT Principles 2016	Civil Law	Common Law
performance)		
Article 7.3.4 (Adequate assurance of due performance)		
Article 7.3.5 (Effects of termination in general)	**§ 325 German Civil Code**	
Article 7.3.6 (Restitution with respect to contracts to be performed at one time)		
Article 7.3.7 (Restitution with respect to long-term contracts)		
Section 4: Damages		
Article 7.4.1 (Right to damages)	**§§ 280 *et seq.* German Civil Code**	
Article 7.4.2 (Full compensation)		
Article 7.4.3 (Certainty of harm)		
Article 7.4.4 (Foreseeability of harm)		
Article 7.4.5 (Proof of harm in case of replacement transaction)		
Article 7.4.6 (Proof of harm by current price)		
Article 7.4.7 (Harm due in part to aggrieved party)	➔ **§ 254 para. 1 German Civil Code**	
Article 7.4.8 (Mitigation of harm)	➔ **§ 254 para. 2 German Civil Code**	
Article 7.4.9 (Interest for failure to pay money)		
Article 7.4.10 (Interest on damages)		
Article 7.4.11 (Manner of monetary redress)		
Article 7.4.12 (Currency in which to assess damages)		
Article 7.4.13 (Agreed payment for non-performance)		

CHAPTER 8: SET-

UNIDROIT Principles 2016	Civil Law	Common Law

OFF

Article 8.1 (Conditions of set-off)	➔ **§ 387 German Civil Code**	
Article 8.2 (Foreign currency set-off)		
Article 8.3 (Set-off by notice)	➔ **§ 388 German Civil Code**	
Article 8.4 (Content of notice)		
Article 8.5 (Effect of set-off)	➔ **§ 389 German Civil Code**	

CHAPTER 9: ASSIGNMENT OF RIGHTS, TRANSFER OF OBLIGATIONS, ASSIGNMENT OF CONTRACTS

Section 1: Assignment of rights

Article 9.1.1 (Definitions)	➔ **§ 398 German Civil Code**	
Article 9.1.2 (Exclusions)	➔ **§§ 399, 400 German Civil Code**	
Article 9.1.3 (Assignability of non-monetary rights)		
Article 9.1.4 (Partial assignment)		
Article 9.1.5 (Future rights)		
Article 9.1.6 (Rights assigned without individual specification)		
Article 9.1.7 (Agreement between assignor and assignee sufficient)	➔ **§ 398 sent. 1 German Civil Code**	
Article 9.1.8 (Obligor's additional costs)		
Article 9.1.9 (Non-assignment clauses)	➔ **§ 399 alt. 2 in conjunction with § 134 German Civil Code, § 354a German Commercial Code**	
Article 9.1.10 (Notice to the obligor)	➔ **§ 407 German Civil Code**	
Article 9.1.11 (Successive assignments)	➔ **§ 408 German Civil Code**	
Article 9.1.12		

71

UNIDROIT Principles 2016	Civil Law	Common Law
(Adequate proof of assignment)		
Article 9.1.13 (Defences and rights of set-off)	➜ **§§ 406, 404 German Civil Code**	
Article 9.1.14 (Rights related to the right assigned)	➜ **§ 401 German Civil Code**	
Article 9.1.15 (Undertakings of the assignor)		
Section 2: Transfer of obligations		
Article 9.2.1 (Modes of transfer)	➜ **§§ 414, 415 German Civil Code**	
Article 9.2.2 (Exclusion)		
Article 9.2.3 (Requirement of obligee's consent to transfer)	➜ **§ 415 German Civil Code**	
Article 9.2.4 (Advance consent of obligee)		
Article 9.2.5 (Discharge of original obligor)		
Article 9.2.6 (Third party performance)	➜ **§ 329 German Civil Code**	
Article 9.2.7 (Defences and rights of set-off)	➜ **§ 417 German Civil Code**	
Article 9.2.8 (Rights related to the obligation transferred)	➜ **§ 418 German Civil Code**	
Section 3: Assignment of contracts		
Article 9.3.1 (Definitions)	➜ **§ 311 para. 1 German Civil Code**	
Article 9.3.2 (Exclusion)		
Article 9.3.3 (Requirement of consent of the other party)		
Article 9.3.4 (Advance consent of the other party)		

UNIDROIT Principles 2016	Civil Law	Common Law
Article 9.3.5 (Discharge of the assignor) **Article 9.3.6** (Defences and rights of set-off) **Article 9.3.7** (Rights transferred with the contract)		

CHAPTER 10: LIMITATION PERIODS

UNIDROIT Principles 2016	Civil Law	Common Law
Article 10.1 (Scope of the Chapter)		
Article 10.2 (Limitation periods)	➔ **§§ 195, 199 para. 3 no. 1 German Civil Code**	
Article 10.3 (Modification of limitation periods by the parties)	➔ **§ 202 German Civil Code**	
Article 10.4 (New limitation period by acknowledgement)	➔ **§ 212 para. 1 no. 1 German Civil Code**	
Article 10.5 (Suspension by judicial proceedings)	➔ **§ 204 para. 1 no. 1 German Civil Code**	
Article 10.6 (Suspension by arbitral proceedings)	➔ **§ 204 para. 1 no. 11 German Civil Code**	
Article 10.7 (Alternative dispute resolution)	➔ **§ 204 para. 1 no. 4 German Civil Code**	
Article 10.8 (Suspension in case of force majeure, death or incapacity)	➔ **§ 206 German Civil Code**	
Article 10.9 (Effects of expiration of limitation period)	➔ **§ 214 German Civil Code**	
Article 10.10 (Right of set-off)	➔ **§ 215 German Civil Code**	
Article 10.11 (Restitution)	➔ **§ 214 para. 1 sent. 1 German Civil Code**	

CHAPTER 11: PLURALITY OF OBLIGORS AND OF OBLIGEES

Section 1: Plurality of obligors

73

UNIDROIT Principles 2016	Civil Law	Common Law
Article 11.1.1 (Definitions)	➔ **§§ 420, 421, 431 German Civil Code**	
Article 11.1.2 (Presumption of joint and several obligations)	➔ **§ 427 German Civil Code**	
Article 11.1.3 (Obligee's rights against joint and several obligors)		
Article 11.1.4 (Availability of defences and rights of set-off)	➔ **§§ 422-425 German Civil Code** ➔ **Art. 1315 French Civil Code**	
Article 11.1.5 (Effect of performance or set-off)	➔ **§ 422 German Civil Code** ➔ **Art. 1313(1) French Civil Code**	
Article 11.1.6 (Effect of release or settlement)	➔ **§ 423 German Civil Code** ➔ **Art. 1313(1) sent. 2 French Civil Code**	➔ **§ 294(1)(b) Restatement 2nd Contracts (USA)**
Article 11.1.7 (Effect of expiration or suspension of limitation period)	➔ **§ 425 German Civil Code**	
Article 11.1.8 (Effect of judgment)	➔ **§ 425 German Civil Code**	
Article 11.1.9 (Apportionment among joint and several obligors)	➔ **§ 426 German Civil Code** ➔ **Art. 178(2) General Rules of the Civil Law of the People's Republic of China** ➔ **Art. 167(1) Turkish Civil Code**	
Article 11.1.10 (Extent of contributory claim)	➔ **§ 426 German Civil Code**	
Article 11.1.11 (Rights of the obligee)	➔ **§§ 426 para. 2, 412 German Civil Code**	
Article 11.1.12 (Defences in contributory claims)		
Article 11.1.13 (Inability to recover)	➔ **§ 426 para. 1 sent. 2 German Civil Code**	
Section 2: Plurality of obligees		
Article 11.2.1 (Definitions)	➔ **§§ 420, 428, 432 German Civil Code**	
Article 11.2.2 (Effects of joint and several claims)	➔ **§ 428 German Civil Code**	

74

UNIDROIT Principles 2016	Civil Law	Common Law
Article 11.2.3 (Availability of defences against joint and several obligees)	➜ **§ 429 para. 3 German Civil Code**	
Article 11.2.4 (Allocation between joint and several obligees)	➜ **§ 430 German Civil Code**	

The UNIDROIT Principles of International Commercial Contracts 2016: A High-Level Analysis for the United States' Commercial Practitioner

Roger E. Barton*

Practitioners in the United States may be unfamiliar with the UNIDROIT Principles of International Commercial Contracts (the "UNIDROIT Principles"), as indeed I was until my good friend Professor Eckart Brödermann of Hamburg, Germany commended them to my attention. They are an amalgam of common and civil law that come together in 211 articles to provide a balanced set of general rules to govern the interpretation and enforcement of international contracts. The UNIDROT Principles have undergone four revisions since they were first published in 1994. In 2007 and again in 2012 the United Nations Commission of International Trade Law (UNCITRAL) endorsed the UNIDROIT Principles to "commend" their use "as appropriate for their intended purposes" which includes their choice as the applicable regime for contracts.

Parties to international commercial agreements may find it advantageous to choose the UNIDROIT Principles as the applicable legal regime to govern their agreements where diverse jurisdictions would otherwise create obligations or curtail rights under an agreement that are unfamiliar or undesirable to the parties. As one would expect, no United States court has ruled substantively on the merits of any specific UNIDROIT Principles; however, US courts have held that arbitration provisions calling for disputes to be resolved under the UNIDROIT Principles or awards rendered pursuant to the UNIDROIT Principles are enforceable absent the normal

* Roger E. Barton, Esq. is the Managing Partner of Barton LLP in New York City

exceptions. Therefore, it may be advisable for US counsel to incorporate the UNIDROIT Principles into an international agreement. To illustrate this point, I have outlined below a few of the leading concepts that will be familiar and important to US parties, but which may not exist if the governing law of a foreign jurisdiction is designated instead of the UNITDROIT Principles.

Good Faith and Fair Dealing as Mandatory Core UNIDROIT Principles pursuant to Articles 1.5 and 1.6(2)

The bedrock US concept of the obligation of good faith and fair dealing as an inherent term contained in every contractual relationship is not present in a number of foreign jurisdictions. For example, the United Kingdom does not recognize such an obligation, and until only recently have courts in parts of Canada adopted what they characterize as "the general organizing principle" of the duty of honest performance, which while similar to the US concept of good faith and fair dealing, is not the same.

Under the UNIDROIT Principles, as in US Common Law, the principle of good faith and fair dealing relates to all phases of a contractual relationship starting with negotiations, Article 2.1.15(2), and continues with 82 references to "reasonableness" as well as other specific references. See also Art. 1.8 which brings the concept of detrimental reliance\estoppel into the UNIDROIT Principles.

Formation of an Agreement – Article 2.1.1 A contract may be concluded by the acceptance of an offer or by conduct of the parties that is sufficient to show an agreement.

Often a contractual provision may be vague or uncertain. In litigation parties will attempt to construe contractual provisions to support their interpretation of the obligations under the contract. Under US Common Law, courts will assess the conduct of the parties as evidence to assist in determining how to interpret and enforce vague contractual provisions. The same is true under the UNIDROIT Principles. Note, however, that acceptance by silence as provided by the UNIDROIT principles is not always the case under US Common Law. A more prolonged course of conduct is generally required.

Merger Clauses – Article 2.1.17 provides that a contract in writing that contains a clause indicating that the writing completely embodies the terms on which the parties have agreed cannot be contradicted or supplemented by evidence of prior statements or agreements. However, such statements or agreements may be used to interpret the writing.

Just as with the concept of interpreting provisions of a contract by course of conduct, courts in the US under Common Law will look to prior communications between the parties to interpret contractual provisions if they are contested by the parties.

It is important to note in this context that the UNIDROIT Principles focus on not **contradicting or supplementing** the contents of the contract and thus, as in US Common Law, they respect and protect the integrity of the written contract. The UNIDROIT Principles, like common law, merely allow for prior writings or statements (parole evidence) to interpret the contract's meaning.

Modification in Particular Form – Article 2.1.18 A contract in writing that contains a clause requiring any modification or termination by agreement to be in a particular form may not be otherwise modified or terminated. However, a party may be precluded by its conduct from asserting such a clause to the extent that the other party has reasonably acted in reliance on that conduct.

Article 2.2.18 reflects the US Common Law principles of:
- detrimental reliance
- equitable estoppel
- good faith\fair dealing

Article 3 – Validity

Grounds for Avoidance

The UNIDROIT Principles have similar concepts for avoidance that are found in the US Common Law. For example: fraud, threat, gross disparity (which is meant to equate to the common law concept of "undue influence" however common law does not go as far as UNIDROIT in terms of giving relief if a party takes unfair economic advantage), and illegality.

Article 3.2.5 – Fraud A party may avoid the contract when it has been led to conclude the contract by the other party's fraudulent representation, including language or practices, or fraudulent non-disclosure of circumstances which, according to reasonable commercial standards of fair dealing, the latter party should have disclosed.

Fraudulent conduct is defined essentially by the same five elements as it is under US Common Law:

1. a material misstatement or omission,
2. made with knowledge or recklessness disregard for the truth,
3. with the intent to deceive the other party,
4. which is relied upon by other party, resulting in
5. damages (actual loss) linked to the misstatement or omission

Fraud is evaluated under UNIDROIT at the same points in the contractual process as under US Common Law:

- Fraudulent inducement (to enter the contract)
- Fraudulent misrepresentation (within the contract)
- Fraudulent performance (under the contract)

The election of remedies under the UNIDROIT Principles applies to all avoidance claims, and again mirrors US Common Law:

- Rescission
- Money damages

80

Article 4 Interpretation

Article 4.1 Intention of the Parties   Under the UNIDROIT Principles, a contract shall be interpreted according to the common intention of the parties. If such an intention cannot be established, the contract shall be interpreted according to the meaning that reasonable persons of the same kind as the parties would give to it in the same circumstances.

US Common Law principles (discussed above) are found in this UNIDROIT Principle which looks to the intention of the parties, their course of conduct and parole evidence.

Importantly, reasonableness is a significant concept under UNIDROIT. As under US Common Law, every contract provision must be interpreted so as to give it reasonable meaning within the context of the overall agreement. Parties often confront this concept in the face of arguments centering on "plain meaning" or "objective meaning" of contract language. This is particularly important in terms of cross-border relationships where strict interpretations of specific words and terms can differ due to language or culture. It is therefore useful to put these words and terms into context and follow a reasonable interpretation that is consistent with the overall intention of the parties to provide reasonable meaning to the contract.

Article 7 Non-Performance
Overall UNIDROIT follows the US Common Law approach to a plurality of remedies including:
- specific performance
- money damages
- Termination rights

  o prior breach excusing subsequent performance
  o frustration of purpose\performance
  o anticipatory breach

- right to cure.

As one can see from the brief analysis of the sections above, UNIDROIT and the US Common Law are more often than not in harmony with one another. Accordingly, it behooves US practitioners to study these principles and to consider drafting international contracts where UNIDROIT is the primary choice of law to govern the agreement.

The UNIDROIT Principles 2016: A Contemporary English Law Perspective

Rina See* and Dharshini Prasad**

I. Introduction

Twenty-five years ago, the first release of the UNIDROIT Principles of International Commercial Contracts ("UNIDROIT Principles" or "Principles") was published in 1994. The UNIDROIT Principles were the result of over two decades of work by independent legal experts from all major legal systems, aiming to produce a "balanced set of rules designed for use throughout the world irrespective of the legal traditions and the economic and political conditions of the countries in which they are to be applied."[1] In this vein, UNIDROIT deliberately avoided seeking endorsements from its member state governments, but aimed for the Principles to be an independent, commercial, non-binding international restatement of general principles of contract law, akin to the US Restatements.[2] And, in the nature of a restatement, rather than simply aiming to reproduce the law, the UNIDROIT Principles "embody what are perceived to be the best solutions, even if still not yet generally adopted."[3]

Reflecting this aim, the Preamble declares that the purpose of the UNIDROIT Principles is to set out general rules for international commercial contracts. Further, the Preamble

---

*   Counsel, Wilmer Cutler Pickering Hale and Dorr LLP.
**   Senior Associate, Wilmer Cutler Pickering Hale and Dorr LLP.
[1]   UNIDROIT Principles 2016 ("UNIDROIT Principles"), Introduction to the 1994 Edition, pp. xxvii-xxix. See also *E. Brödermann*, UNIDROIT Principles of International Commercial Contracts: An Article-by-Article Commentary (2018), pp. 5-6.
[2]   UNIDROIT Principles, Introduction to the 1994 Edition, p. xxix.
[3]   UNIDROIT Principles, Introduction to the 1994 Edition, p. xxix. See also *R. Goode*, "International Restatements of Contract and English Contract Law" (1997) 2 Unif. L. Rev 231, 234 ("…the task of those engaged in the work of harmonisation, whether it takes the form of a convention, a set of uniform rules to be incorporated by contract, a model law or a scholarly restatement, is to find the best solutions to typical problems, and thus to improve the law, not merely to reproduce it.").

envisages that the Principles will be applied to govern contracts either by the parties' choice, or as default rules where parties have agreed that their contract should be governed by "general principles of law," "*lex mercatoria*" or the like, or have simply not made provision for an applicable law. Finally, the Principles can also be used to interpret or supplement international uniform law instruments or domestic law and may serve as a model for national and international legislators.

Now in its fourth release, the UNIDROIT Principles of International Commercial Contracs 2016 have been cited and applied in many court and arbitral decisions around the world, and spawns numerous articles, texts and commentaries. Recently, the merits of utilizing the Principles in international commercial contracts arising out of China's Belt and Road Initiative were discussed at a conference held by the Chinese European Arbitration Centre in September 2018, as a way of finding common ground between disparate civil and common legal traditions.[4] This article thus considers the UNIDROIT Principles' applicability and utility from an English common law perspective.

The UNIDROIT Principles successfully capture general concepts of contract law common to legal systems around the world. To the extent the UNIDROIT Principles are – to use the words of Sir Roy Goode – "non-normative and therefore pose no threat to national law but are available as a resource to courts, arbitral tribunals and legislators,"[5] they have undoubtedly been a great success. The Principles have been referred to in court decisions from all over the world, including by the highest courts in the United Kingdom, Singapore, Australia, and New Zealand.[6] The Principles are also a common reference point in comparative law exercises. For English lawyers, the

---

[4] One of the authors, Dharshini Prasad, was a panelist on this topic at the conference.

[5] *R. Goode*, "Insularity or Leadership? The Role of the United Kingdom in the Harmonisation of Commercial Law" (2001) 50 ICLQ 751, 763.

[6] See, e.g., MWB Business Exchange Centres Ltd v Rock Advertising Ltd [2018] UKSC 24 (English Sup. Ct.), [13], [16]; Sembcorp Marine Ltd v PPL Holdings Pte Ltd [2013] SGCA 43 (Singapore Ct. App.), [37]; Koompahtoo Local Aboriginal Land Council v Sanpine Pty Ltd [2007] HCA 61 (Aust. High Ct.), [108]; Vector Gas Ltd v Bay of Plenty Energy Ltd [2010] NZSC 5 (N.Z. Sup. Ct.), [20].

foundational principles of freedom of contract and the binding nature of contract are easily recognizable,[7] as are the techniques of offer and acceptance in contract formation and the doctrines of mistake and illegality in contract validity.[8] The concepts of express and implied obligations, third party rights, set-off, assignment, termination, damages and specific performance all broadly have counterparts in both the UNIDROIT Principles and English law.

Yet, despite being a "system of rules especially tailored to the need of international commercial transactions,"[9] and despite the commonalities captured by the UNIDROIT Principles, international commercial parties have been hesitant to adopt the UNIDROIT Principles in their contracts.[10] In 2017, for example, of the 810 new cases filed with the ICC, only one contract expressly provided for the application of the UNIDROIT Principles.[11] In contrast, English law remains one of the most popular applicable laws chosen for international commercial contracts, coming in top in statistics released by major arbitral institutions such as the ICC,[12] LCIA[13] and SIAC.[14]

Why have commercial parties been so hesitant to apply the UNIDROIT Principles to their contracts – even in international commercial arbitrations, where non-national choices of law are

---

[7] UNIDROIT Principles, Arts. 1.1 and 1.3.

[8] UNIDROIT Principles, Chs. 2-3. See S. Lake, "An Empirical Study of the UNIDROIT Principles – International and British Response" (2011) 16 Rev. dr. unif. 669, 685.

[9] UNIDROIT Principles, Introduction to the 1994 Edition, pp. xxvii-xxix.

[10] See, e.g., G. Born, International Commercial Arbitration (2d ed, 2014), pp. 2766-2767 ("In general, commercial parties have been reluctant to adopt the UNIDROIT Principles, notwithstanding the quality of the efforts devoted to them.") This reluctance is particularly pronounced for those from the English law tradition: see S. Lake, "An Empirical Study of the UNIDROIT Principles – International and British Response" (2011) 16 Rev. dr. unif. 669, 671-677.

[11] ICC, 2017 ICC Dispute Resolution Statistics (2018) 2 ICC Bull., pp. 52 and 61.

[12] ICC, 2017 ICC Dispute Resolution Statistics (2018) 2 ICC Bull., p. 61 (87% of disputes referred to the ICC in 2017 included a choice-of-law clause, and of these, the laws of England US states were the most frequent choices).

[13] LCIA, Facts and Figures – 2017 Casework Report (2018), p. 9 (English law was the applicable law in 85% of LCIA arbitrations in 2017).

[14] SIAC, Annual Report 2017 (2018), p. 20 (94% of disputes referred to SIAC in 2017 included a choice-of-law clause, and of these, Singapore law was the most popular applicable law (61%), followed by English law (21%)).

permitted? Michael Joachim Bonell, who chaired the Working Group for the UNIDROIT Principles, observes that, as a soft law instrument, the UNIDROIT Principles' application is currently limited in practice because they are "binding only within the limits of party autonomy, whereas in the absence of voluntary acceptance by the parties, courts and arbitral tribunals will apply them, if at all, only if persuaded by their intrinsic merits."[15] On a practical level, parties are likely to be dissuaded by the uncertainty of how such a choice would be received and applied compared to a national law, especially given the relatively limited jurisprudence and precedent accompanying the Principles.[16] In contrast, legal systems commonly used in international commercial transactions, such as English, American, French and German law, benefit from jurisprudence that spans hundreds of years.

In the authors' view, one of the main reasons for the UNIDROIT Principles' limited reception in commercial practice amongst English lawyers, lawyers from other common law jurisdictions that share a heritage with English law and parties familiar with English law is a foundational conceptual difference between the Principles and the English legal tradition: namely, the role of good faith and fair dealing against the principle of party autonomy. While the principle of good faith is a theme running through the UNIDROIT Principles and one familiar to many major legal systems, it is, as yet, foreign to English law. Indeed, in the authors' view, it is a compelling reason explaining the English common lawyer's reflexive wariness of applying the UNIDROIT Principles in practice. The desire to default to familiar legal concepts may also explain the sustained popularity of English law as a choice of national law amongst English lawyers and lawyers from other common law jurisdictions that share a heritage with English law.

Section II below discusses the role of good faith in the UNIDROIT Principles as compared to its position under English law. That fundamental conceptual distinction manifests itself in

---

[15] *M. J. Bonell*, "Symposium Paper: The UNIDROIT Principles of International Commercial Contracts: Achievements in Practice and Prospects for the Future" (2010) 17 Austl. Int'l L.J. 177, 181.

[16] *G. Born*, International Commercial Arbitration (2d ed., 2014), pp. 2766-2767.

other differences between the UNIDROIT Principles and English common law, and examples of this are given in Section III. Despite this conceptual difference, however, as discussed in Section IV, the slow but persistent trend in common law jurisdictions, including England, to recognize good faith in contract law, together with the increasing level of trade and commerce between parties from different legal traditions – as evidenced, for instance, in China's Belt and Road initiative – may well lead to the Principles achieving greater acceptance in the years to come amongst those from the English common law tradition.

II. The Concept of "Good faith" in English Common Law and the Unidroit Principles

Most civil legal systems recognize an overriding doctrine of good faith in commercial relations. The French Civil Code, for example, provides that "[c]ontracts must be negotiated, formed and performed in good faith," and deems this a matter of public policy.[17] Other civil codes, including that of the People's Republic of China, contain similar provisions.[18] A general good-faith doctrine is also well-established in many common law jurisdictions. In many US states, the Uniform Commercial Code provides that "every contract or duty within the Uniform Commercial Code imposes an obligation of good faith in its performance and enforcement."[19] This principle is also expressed in the *Restatement (Second) of Contracts*.[20]

---

[17] French Civil Code, Art. 1104.
[18] Swiss Code of Obligations, Art. 2 ("Every person must act in good faith in the exercise of his or her rights and in the performance of his or her obligations."); German Civil Code, § 242 ("An obligor has a duty to perform according to the requirements of good faith, taking customary practice into consideration."); Contract Law of the People's Republic of China, Arts. 6 ("The parties shall abide by the principle of good faith in exercising their rights and performing their obligations.") and 60(2) ("The parties shall fully perform their respective obligations in accordance with the contract. The parties shall abide by the principle of good faith, and perform obligations such as notification, assistance, and confidentiality, etc. in light of the nature and purpose of the contract and in accordance with the relevant usage.").
[19] Uniform Commercial Code, § 1-304.
[20] American Law Institute, Restatement (Second) of Contracts (1981), § 205.

It is perhaps no surprise then that the drafters of the UNIDROIT Principles chose to expressly state the "general duty of the parties to act in accordance with good faith and fair dealing and, in a number of specific instances, imposing standards of reasonable behaviour."[21] Art. 1.7(1) of the UNIDROIT Principles provides that "[e]ach party must act in accordance with good faith and fair dealing in international trade," while Art 1.7(2) prevents the parties from excluding or limiting this duty. The concept of good faith and fair dealing forms the basis of many provisions in the Principles. As the Official Comment to Art. 1.7 notes, "good faith and fair dealing may be considered to be one of the fundamental ideas underlying the Principles."[22]

Yet such a conception of good faith and fair dealing does not exist in English contract law. As one English Court of Appeal case put it:
"There is no general doctrine of good faith in the English law of contract. The plaintiffs are free to act as they wish, provided they do not act in breach of a term of the contract."[23]

The deep-seated nature of this sentiment in English law can also be seen in the strong reactions evoked by the English High Court decision of *Yam Seng Pte Ltd v International Trade Corporation Ltd*.[24] In that case, Leggatt J held that there was an implied duty that the parties to a distribution agreement would deal in good faith with each other and suggested that such an implied duty could exist in English law in certain factual circumstances. But even this limited encroachment on the "traditional English hostility" toward a doctrine of good faith was controversial: what may not be readily apparent to observers from other legal traditions is why.

---

[21] UNIDROIT Principles, Introduction to the 1994 Edition, p. xxix.
[22] UNIDROIT Principles, Art. 1.7, Comment 1.
[23] James Spencer & Co Ltd v Tame Valley Padding Co Ltd [1997] EWCA Civ 2288.
[24] Yam Seng Pte Ltd v International Trade Corporation Ltd [2013] EWHC 111 (QB). See Leggatt J, "Contractual Duties of Good Faith", Lecture to the Commercial Bar Association, 18 October 2016, para. 3 ("I am not intending this evening to repeat or discuss what I said in the Yam Seng case. It has tended to evoke quite strong reactions – whether positive or negative.").

As discussed in *Yam Seng*,[25] the main reasons underlying the opposition towards a general good faith doctrine are threefold. First, the principle of freedom of contract is dominant in English law. It embodies an "ethos of individualism," where each party is free to pursue its own self-interest but is also obliged to protect itself under the *caveat emptor* principle. Second, unlike civil systems based on codified law, English common law proceeds incrementally and factually through case law rather than applying general principles. Bingham L.J. famously encapsulated this idea in his comment that "English law has, characteristically, committed itself to no such overriding principle [of good faith] but has developed piecemeal solutions in response to demonstrated problems of unfairness."[26] Third, introducing a standard of good faith is thought to create a level of subjectivity and uncertainty that is antithetical to the foundational importance of certainty in English law. As Sir Roy Goode once put it, under English law, "the predictability of the legal outcome of a case is more important than absolute justice."[27]

Rather than being opposed to the idea of good faith *per se*, English law's rejection of this general concept stems from its conflict with fundamental notions inherent to English law. Indeed, the concept itself is unfamiliar for English common lawyers, leading Sir Roy Goode to quip that "we do not know quite what it means."[28] Attempts to introduce a general doctrine of good faith in English law have been resisted. One Court of Appeal judgment reiterated that "there is no general doctrine of 'good faith' in English contract law," but acknowledged that a duty of good faith could be implied by law as an incident of certain categories of contract.[29] In another recent Court of Appeal decision, Moore-Bick L.J. stated:

---

[25] Yam Seng Pte Ltd v International Trade Corporation Ltd [2013] EWHC 111 (QB), para. 123.

[26] Interfoto Picture Library Ltd v Stilletto Visual Programmes Ltd [1989] 1 Q.B. 433, 439.

[27] R. Goode, "The Concept of 'Good Faith' in English Law" (Rome, 1992).

[28] R. Goode, "The Concept of 'Good Faith' in English Law" (Rome, 1992).

[29] Mid Essex Hospital Services NHS Trust v Compass Group UK and Ireland Ltd (t/a Medirest) [2013] EWCA Civ 200, para. 105. But see Greenclose Ltd v National Westminster Bank Plc [2014] EWHC 1156 (Ch), para. 150 ("[T]here is no general doctrine of good faith in English contract law and such a term is unlikely to arise

"In my view the better course is for the law to develop along established lines rather than to encourage judges to look for what the judge in this case called some 'general organising principle' drawn from cases of disparate kinds. ... There is in my view a real danger that if a general principle of good faith were established it would be invoked as often to undermine as to support the terms in which the parties have reached agreement."[30]

Similar views have been expressed in other Commonwealth jurisdictions that follow the English common law. For example, the Singapore Court of Appeal in *Ng Giap Hon v Westcomb Securities Pte Ltd* has commented that "[t]he doctrine of good faith is very much a fledgling doctrine in English and (most certainly) Singapore contract law."[31] It expressed concern that "even in the academic literature (which has witnessed the most discussion as well as analysis of the doctrine), there are differing views as to what the doctrine of good faith means as well as how it is to be applied." In New Zealand, while there is judicial support for the doctrine,[32] it was recognized that "the courts have not yet incorporated the doctrine of good faith into our law."[33] And while there is authority pointing towards recognition of a general principle of good faith in Australia and Canada, the scope and meaning of such a principle is not settled.[34]

---

by way of necessary implication in a contract between two sophisticated commercial parties negotiating at arms' length.").

[30] MSC Mediterranean Shipping Company S.A. v Cottonex Anstalt [2016] EWCA Civ 789, para. 45.

[31] Ng Giap Hon v Westcomb Securities Pte Ltd [2009] SGCA 19, para. 47. See also The One Suites Pte Ltd v Pacific Motor Credit (Pte) Ltd [2015] SGCA 21, para. 44, declining to decide definitively on the issue of whether there is a duty to cooperate and its relationship to doctrines of good faith.

[32] See Bobux Marketing Ltd v Raynor Marketing Ltd [2001] NZCA 348, para. [48] (Thomas J, dissenting) ("I have elsewhere noted the void in the law due to the absence of a developed doctrine of good faith.").

[33] Gibbons Holdings Ltd v Wholesale Distributors Ltd [2007] NZSC 37, para. 149.

[34] See, e.g., Royal Botanic Gardens and Domain Trust v South Sydney City Council [2002] HCA 5 (declining to comment on the emerging authorities on the existence and cope of a duty of good faith); Bhasin v Hrynew 2014 SCC 71, para. 93 (recognizing a general organizing principle of good faith and a new common law duty of honest performance as a manifestation of that organizing principle).

Importantly, the conception of good faith itself differs in different jurisdictions. Leggatt J, writing extrajudicially in support of a principle of good faith in English law, noted that in *Yam Seng* he had not sufficiently recognized that there were two different conceptions of good faith: in civil law systems, good faith applies to the negotiation and formation of contracts and cannot be excluded by the parties as a matter of public policy, whereas in common law systems, the duty of good faith only exists in the performance of a contract and can be excluded or limited by the parties.[35] All discussions of good faith in the common law context – including in the US, UK, Australia, Canada and Singapore – refer to the latter concept, not the former.

The UNIDROIT Principles' conception of good faith, in contrast, more closely reflects those of civil law regimes. As noted above, Art. 1.7 imposes an obligation on parties to act in accordance with good faith and fair dealing generally, not just in the performance of contracts. It also prevents exclusion or limitation of this duty. An illustrative application of this point can be found in Art. 2.1.15 on negotiations in bad faith. Art. 2.1.15(2) provides that "a party who negotiates or breaks off negotiations in bad faith is liable for the losses caused to the other party," and Art. 2.1.15(3) explains that "[i]t is bad faith ... for a party to enter into or continue negotiations when intending not to reach an agreement with the other party." This is a foreign concept to English law, which takes a very circumscribed view of the obligations that can exist between the parties before a contract is formed. Under English law, for example, save where an estoppel arises, it is acceptable for a party to arbitrarily break off negotiations at any stage or negotiate in parallel with several different parties without informing any of them.[36]

---

[35] *Leggatt J*, "Contractual Duties of Good Faith", Lecture to the Commercial Bar Association, 18 October 2016, paras. 4-10. While there is no general duty of good faith in English common law, principles like estoppel and unconscionability arguably reflect aspects of good faith obligations, albeit in limited terms. See e.g. J. Carter, Carter's Breach of Contract (2012), pp. 492-499.

[36] *R. Goode*, "The Concept of 'Good Faith' in English Law" (Rome, 1992) ("We do not therefore recognize that the opening of negotiations for a contract by itself creates any sort of duty relationship. We take the view that both parties are at risk until a contract is actually formed. Therefore we see nothing wrong in a party who is conducting negotiations arbitrarily breaking them off, even if he has brought the

The fundamental differences between English law and the UNIDROIT Principles – both in the existence and scope of the principle of good faith – is, in the authors' view, an important impediment in English law to the acceptance of the UNIDROIT Principles. As the next section demonstrates, the wide influence of the concept of good faith on other provisions in the UNIDROIT Principles has led to divergent approaches from English contract law.

III. Manifestations of "Good Faith" in the UNIDROIT Principles

As noted in the Official Comment to Art. 1.7, the principle of good faith is a fundamental idea underlying the UNIDROIT Principles. In fact, the comment lists no less than 37 provisions in the Principles that are direct or indirect applications of the principle of good faith. Many of the disparities between the UNIDROIT Principles and English contract law can, in the authors' view, be explained by their respective positions on the notion of good faith. This section focuses on three main areas: (a) contractual interpretation and the role of extrinsic evidence; (b) the effect of changed circumstances and hardship; and (c) the concept of cure.

1. Contractual Interpretation and Extrinsic Evidence

One well-known difference between the civil and common law is their approach to contractual interpretation. While civil law regimes focus on ascertaining the subjective intention of the contracting parties, common law approaches focus on the wording of the contract and what they would convey to a reasonable person having the background knowledge of the contracting parties. Again, the objective approach that English

---

other party to the brink of the contract, just about to sign it. Also we see nothing wrong in a party conducting negotiations in parallel with several parties, without telling any party that he is negotiating with the others.").

law adopts reflects its emphasis on certainty, regardless of what the parties may have in fact subjectively intended.

In what is considered an indirect application of the principle of good faith,[37] Arts. 4.1 and 4.2 set out the UNIDROIT Principles' approach to contractual interpretation. They provide for two distinct approaches and the relationship between them:
First, "[a] contract shall be interpreted according to the common intention of the parties," and if the statements and conduct of one party is concerned, it should be interpreted "according to that party's intention if the other party knew or could not have been unaware of that intention."[38]

Second, if the parties' common intention or one party's intention cannot be established, the contract, statement or other conduct is to be interpreted "according to the meaning that [a] reasonable person[s] of the same kind as the [parties or other party] would give to it in the same circumstances."[39]

Art. 4.3 then provides that:
"In applying Articles 4.1 and 4.2, regard shall be had to all the circumstances, including
(a)   preliminary negotiations between the parties;
(b)   practices which the parties have established between themselves;
(c)   the conduct of the parties subsequent to the conclusion of the contract;
(d)   the nature and purpose of the contract;
(e)   the meaning commonly given to terms and expressions in the trade concerned;
(f)   usages."

Two points are worth noting. First, the primary approach under the Principles is the "subjective" approach familiar to civil law systems: the aim is to identify what the parties subjectively intended, rather than what the parties must have intended on an

---

[37] See UNIDROIT Principles, Art. 1.7, Comment 1. See also *P. Finn*, "Symposium Paper: The UNIDROIT Principles: An Australian Perspective" (2010) 17 Austl. Int'l L.J. 193, 196.
[38] UNIDROIT Principles, Arts. 4.1(1) and 4.2(1).
[39] UNIDROIT Principles, Arts. 4.1(2) and 4.2(2).

objective basis, assessed from the perspective of a reasonable person with knowledge of the relevant factual matrix. Second, the UNIDROIT Principles depart from the traditional English law orthodoxy that evidence of preliminary negotiations and subsequent conduct are inadmissible in interpreting or varying written contracts.[40] Art. 4.3 expressly **requires** regard to be had to all relevant circumstances, **including** preliminary negotiations and subsequent conduct, and as such rejects the parol evidence rule. Both are uncommon concepts for English common lawyers, who have become adept at discarding "irrelevant" subjective evidence of intention in the pursuit of objective meaning.

The Official Comment to Art. 4.1 observes that while the "common intention" approach is to prevail, the practical importance of this is not to be overstated, because the subjective and objective intentions of the parties usually coincide, and there are usually evidential difficulties in establishing a true common intention.[41] Similarly, commentary on this provision contends that "the conflict between these two ideal-type approaches rarely matters in practice and it has largely been overcome in modern legal systems."[42] It argues that consistent with the international trend, Art. 4.1 in fact "merges 'subjective' and 'objective' approaches to contractual interpretation" by requiring "objective" criteria to be taken into account in ascertaining the parties' common intention, while "subjectivizing" the reasonableness standard by requiring regard to the circumstances in which the parties operated.[43]

Nevertheless, courts in the English common law tradition have not generally regarded the UNIDROIT Principles as reflecting

---

[40] See, e.g., Investors Compensation Scheme Ltd v West Bromwich Building Society [1998] 1 WLR 896, 913; Chartbrook Ltd v Persimmon Homes Ltd [2009] UKHL 38, para. 39.
[41] UNIDROIT Principles, Art. 4.1, Comment 1.
[42] *S. Vogenauer* (ed.), Commentary on the UNIDROIT Principles of International Commercial Contracts (PICC) (2d ed., 2015), p. 580.
[43] *S. Vogenauer* (ed.), Commentary on the UNIDROIT Principles of International Commercial Contracts (PICC) (2d ed., 2015), p. 581. See also E. Brödermann, UNIDROIT Principles of International Commercial Contracts: An Article-by-Article Commentary (2018), p. 110 ("The Principles (i) on contract interpretation … and (ii) on interpretation of statements and other conduct … provide a common ground merging these different approaches….").

any trend towards a unified approach; nor have they accepted the UNIDROIT Principles as consistent with English law, particularly on the role of prior negotiations and subsequent conduct in contractual interpretation. In the leading case of *Chartbrook Ltd v Persimmon Homes Ltd*,[44] Lord Hoffman noted that the UNIDROIT Principles "reflect the French philosophy of contractual interpretation, which is altogether different from that of English law. ... One cannot in my opinion simply transpose rules based on one philosophy of contractual interpretation to another, or assume that the practical effect of admitting such evidence under the English system of civil procedure will be the same as that under a Continental system."[45]

As Lord Hoffman explained, unlike the UNIDROIT Principles and continental legal systems where evidence of the parties' negotiating history and conduct is highly relevant to ascertaining the parties' (actual) common intention, such evidence is largely irrelevant and potentially unhelpful under English law because English law is only concerned with what the final contract means to a reasonable person in the parties' position.[46] Under this objective approach, admitting such evidence would also create greater uncertainty and increase the cost of legal advice and proceedings.[47] Even if this exclusionary rule means that the full picture is not presented, as Lord Hoffman put it, this "may be justified in the more general interest of economy and predictability in obtaining advice and adjudicating disputes," especially if parties are accustomed to carefully reading their agreements before signing them.[48] The House of Lords therefore reaffirmed the rule that pre-contractual negotiations are inadmissible as evidence of the parties' contractual intentions.

This sentiment has been echoed in various other Commonwealth jurisdictions, even where the rule against extrinsic evidence has been relaxed. In New Zealand, in the Supreme Court decision of *Vector Gas Ltd v Bay of Plenty*

---

44   Chartbrook Ltd v Persimmon Homes Ltd [2009] UKHL 38, para. 39.
45   Chartbrook Ltd v Persimmon Homes Ltd [2009] UKHL 38, para. 39.
46   See Chartbrook Ltd v Persimmon Homes Ltd [2009] UKHL 38, paras. 28-41.
47   Chartbrook Ltd v Persimmon Homes Ltd [2009] UKHL 38, paras. 35-38.
48   Chartbrook Ltd v Persimmon Homes Ltd [2009] UKHL 38, para. 41.

Energy Ltd, Tipping J rejected that evidence of subjective intention alone was admissible, despite ultimately finding that prior negotiations were admissible to establish the surrounding circumstances against which the interpretive exercise is to be conducted.[49]   To this end, his Honor distinguished the UNIDROIT Principles' approach of allowing reference to preliminary negotiations on the basis that the French approach was heavily influential in its drafting, noting that "that is not the common law way."[50]   In Singapore, the Court of Appeal in *Sembcorp Marine Ltd v PPL Holdings Pte Ltd* described the UNIDROIT Principles as reflecting the "robust approach" towards the admissibility of extrinsic evidence. It noted that due to the role of Singapore's Evidence Act and differences between the common law adversarial process and the civil law inquisitorial process, careful examination is required before such an approach is adopted."[51]

Whether these comments correctly describe the UNIDROIT Principles as reflecting a civil law over a common law approach is, ultimately, immaterial for these purposes. What they show is the perception that there is a conceptual and practical divide between the English common law of contract and the UNIDROIT Principles. This stems from juridical differences on the purpose of contractual interpretation, the role of the parties in contending for a particular interpretation, and the evidence permitted to do so – bearing in mind differences also in procedural expectations due to differing attitudes to discovery and document disclosure. On the whole, common law parties do not see themselves as bound in good faith to a contractual interpretation that they may have subjectively intended at the time of contracting, and it is accordingly permissible to rely on evidence and evidential rules to contend for a different interpretation on the wording of the contract. There would arguably need to be a shift in perception before parties accustomed to English common law principles can adopt the UNIDROIT Principles' approach to contractual interpretation in practice.

---

[49]   Vector Gas Ltd v Bay of Plenty Energy Ltd [2010] NZSC 5, paras. 20, 27-37.
[50]   Vector Gas Ltd v Bay of Plenty Energy Ltd [2010] NZSC 5, fn. 17.
[51]   Sembcorp Marine Ltd v PPL Holdings Pte Ltd [2013] SGCA 43, paras. 37-38.

2. Changes in Circumstances and Hardship

Another illustration of the role of good faith in the UNIDROIT Principles is the provision on hardship, a concept that has no counterpart in English law (and indeed, other common and civil law systems) and which have been described as "[t]he most radical provisions of the Principles."[52]   Essentially, Art. 6.2.3 permits a disadvantaged party suffering hardship to request renegotiation of the contract, and if there is a failure to reach agreement, to resort to the court, which may, if reasonable, terminate or adapt the contract. Hardship is defined in Art. 6.2.2 as "where the occurrence of events fundamentally alters the equilibrium of the contract either because the cost of a party's performance has increased or because the value of the performance a party receives has diminished," and must satisfy four requirements: (a) the events must occur or become known after the conclusion of the contract; (b) the events could not reasonably have been taken into account by the disadvantaged party; (c) the events are beyond the control of the disadvantaged party; and (d) the risk must not have been assumed by the disadvantaged party.

Although few legal systems recognize a doctrine entitled "hardship,"[53] the provisions on hardship bear some similarity to civil law concepts such as *Wegfall der Geschäftsgrundlage*, *imprévision* and *eccessiva onerosità sopravvenuta*.[54]   Several

---

[52] *R. Goode*, "International Restatements of Contract and English Contract Law" (1997) 2 Unif. L. Rev 231, 243. See also E. Brödermann, UNIDROIT Principles of International Commercial Contracts: An Article-by-Article Commentary (2018), pp. 176-177, describing the hardship provisions as "an innovative general (default) concept (which may be subject to more specific contractual provisions...)."

[53] *S. Vogenauer* (ed.), Commentary on the UNIDROIT Principles of International Commercial Contracts (PICC) (2d ed., 2015), p. 808.

[54] See UNIDROIT Principles, Art. 6.2.1, Comment 2 ("The phenomenon of hardship has been acknowledged by various legal systems under the guise of other concepts such as frustration of purpose, Wegfall der Geschäftsgrundlage, imprévision, eccessiva onerosità sopravvenuta, etc.")

continental legal systems allow contracts to be varied or adapted by the courts following a change in circumstances.[55]

The US recognizes a doctrine of impracticability, where non-performance of a contract is excused if performance has become impractical due to a contingency or supervening event,[56] and there is some authority (albeit limited) for courts altering contractual obligations rather than simply discharging the contract.[57] In contrast, as explained below, in many English common law systems, the "all-or-nothing" doctrine of frustration is the only means of escaping a contract where circumstances have changed.[58]

Frustration under English contract law requires the change in circumstance to cause performance to be "radically different" from what was undertaken in the contract – mere hardship, inconvenience or material loss is insufficient.[59] The doctrine has been described as follows:

> "Frustration of a contract takes place when there **supervenes an event (without default of either party and for which the contract makes no sufficient provision)** which **so significantly changes the nature (not merely the expense or onerousness)** of the outstanding contractual rights and/or obligations **from what the parties could reasonably have contemplated** at the time of its execution that it would be unjust to hold them to the literal sense of its stipulations in the new circumstances; in such case **the law declares both parties to be discharged from further performance**."[60]

---

[55] See, e.g., German Civil Code, § 313 (Störung der Geschäftsgrundlage); French Civil Code, Art. 1195; Italian Civil Code, Art. 1467; Dutch Civil Code, Art. 6:258; Austrian Civil Code, §§ 936, 1052, 1170a et seq.

[56] See Uniform Commercial Code, § 2-615(a) (excuse by failure of presupposed conditions); American Law Institute, Restatement (Second) of Contracts (1981), § 261 (discharge by supervening impracticality).

[57] See, e.g., Aluminum Corp of America v Essex Group, Inc. 499 F Supp 53 (1980) (court adjusted price in long term service contract where production costs rose beyond foreseeable limits of risk).

[58] See G. Treitel, Frustration and Force Majeure (3d ed., 2014), paras. 6-021-6-028.

[59] Davis Contractors Ltd v Fareham Urban District Council [1956] UKHL 3, [1956] A.C. 696, 729.

[60] National Carriers Ltd v Panalpina (Northern) Ltd [1981] A.C. 675, 700.

The English authorities on frustration have been adopted in several other Commonwealth jurisdictions, including Australia, New Zealand and Singapore.[61]

In substance, although "hardship" itself does not frustrate a contract, the tests for establishing frustration in English common law jurisdictions and hardship under the Principles are broadly comparable, both requiring a fundamental or radical change brought about by an unforeseeable and uncontrollable event for which the parties did not provide. The novelty of the Principles' hardship provisions lies in its consequences: under English law, if frustration is established, the contract is automatically terminated and the parties are discharged. There is no opportunity for the court to adjust the parties' obligations. The suggestion by Denning L.J. (as he then was) that a court could do what is "just and reasonable" in the new circumstances was rejected by the House of Lords;[62] it is said that this test gives too much discretion to the court and ignores the limited data for the court's decision.[63] While there has been statutory intervention in the area of frustration in several common law jurisdictions, these do not give courts the power to adjust the contract to new circumstances.[64]

The English law position on the consequences of frustration ultimately boils down to promoting certainty. The existence of a judicial discretion to alter a contract could impose on the parties a bargain that the parties had never anticipated; a concept that English contract law abhors. To escape the potentially harsh effects of the frustration doctrine, hardship or adaptation clauses are frequently inserted in commercial contracts; indeed, these hardship clauses inspired the hardship provisions in the Principles.[65] However, the theoretical basis for including a

---

[61] See, e.g., Codelfa Construction Pty. Ltd. v State Rail Authority of N.S.W. [1982] HCA 24; (1982) 149 CLR 337; Planet Kids Limited v Auckland Council [2013] NZSC 147; [2014] 1 NZLR 149; Alliance Concrete Singapore Pte Ltd v Sato Kogyo (S) Pte Ltd [2014] SGCA 35.

[62] British Movietonews Ltd v London & District Cinemas Ltd [1952] A.C. 166.

[63] H. Beale, Chitty on Contracts (33d ed., 2018), para. 23-008.

[64] See, e.g., Law Reform (Frustrated Contracts) Act 1943 (UK); Contract and Commercial Law Act 2017 (NZ), ss. 60-69; Frustrated Contracts Act (SG).

[65] See UNIDROIT Principles, Art. 6.2.1, Comment 2; E. Brödermann, UNIDROIT Principles of International Commercial Contracts: An Article-by-Article

hardship clause in contracts is very different from its presence in default contractual rules. While the former is an exercise of the parties' autonomy, the latter reflects a duty of good faith, constraining the parties' behavior by directing a process of renegotiation and contract adaptation in the event of hardship.

The hardship provisions in the UNIDROIT Principles are thus not easy to reconcile with the English law attitude to contract. As Sir Roy Goode observed, from an English court's perspective, the fact that hardship clauses are often included in international commercial contracts does not lend weight to the court's power to do so: to the contrary, it suggests that "if parties choose not to insert into their contract hardship clauses which are common form in other contracts, they cannot complain if they are held to their bargain and may, indeed, be considered to have impliedly accepted the risks involved."[66] This is thus another example of how good faith in the UNIDROIT Principles can create expectations of conduct that are less familiar to English common lawyers.

3. The Concept of Cure

The third example of a manifestation of good faith in the UNIDROIT Principles is the provision on "cure by non-performing party" in Art. 7.1.4, which, again, has no equivalent under English law. This provides:

(1)   The non-performing party may, at its own expense, cure any non-performance, provided that
   (a)   Without undue delay, it gives notice indicating the proposed manner and timing of the cure;
   (b)   Cure is appropriate in the circumstances;
   (c)   The aggrieved party has no legitimate interest in refusing cure; and
   (d)   Cure is effected promptly.
(2)   The right to cure is not precluded by notice of termination.

Commentary (2018), p. 176; *S. Vogenauer* (ed.), Commentary on the UNIDROIT Principles of International Commercial Contracts (PICC) (2d ed., 2015), p. 808.

[66]   *R. Goode*, "International Restatements of Contract and English Contract Law" (1997) 2 Unif. L. Rev 231, 244.

(3)   Upon effective notice of cure, rights of the aggrieved party that are inconsistent with the non-performing party's performance are suspended until the time for cure has expired.

(4)   The aggrieved party may withhold performance pending cure.

(5)   Notwithstanding cure, the aggrieved party retains the right to claim damages for delay as well as for any harm caused or not prevented by the cure.

As the Official Comment notes, Art. 7.1.4 reflects the policies of contract preservation, economic waste minimization/mitigation of harm, and good faith.[67] While the broad ability to cure non-performance is recognized in many jurisdictions, including Germany and the US, precise procedural requirements differ – such as whether it is the non-conforming or the aggrieved party that has the right to demand cure and whether the right to cure is precluded by termination of the contract.[68]

While it is controversial whether English contract law recognizes the concept of cure generally,[69] it is clear that English law on discharge by breach bears little resemblance to Art. 7.1.4 of the Principles.   Under English law, absent agreement otherwise, where a breach of contract amounts to a repudiatory breach,[70] the innocent party is given the right to elect whether to affirm the contract and continue to be bound by it, or to terminate the

---

[67] UNDROIT Principles, Art. 7.1.4, Comment 1. See also E. Brödermann, UNIDROIT Principles of International Commercial Contracts: An Article-by-Article Commentary (2018), pp. 191-192.

[68] See S. Vogenauer (ed.), Commentary on the UNIDROIT Principles of International Commercial Contracts (PICC) (2d ed., 2015), pp. 845-846. See, e.g., German Civil Code, §§ 439 and 635; Dutch Civil Code, Art. 6:82; Uniform Commercial Code, § 2-508.

[69] See, e.g., R. Goode, "International Restatements of Contract and English Contract Law" (1997) 2 Unif. L. Rev 231, 242.

[70] A repudiatory breach giving rise to a discharge of contract can arise by (a) renunciation of the contract; (b) impossibility created by one party; and (c) total or partial failure of performance: see, e.g., Heyman v Darwins Ltd [1942] AC 356, 397. For the position grounds for termination for non-performance in Singapore, see RDC Concrete Pte Ltd v Sato Kogyo (S) Pte Ltd [2007] SGCA 39.

contract.[71]   There is no obligation on the innocent party to give the non-performing party further time to perform or to cure its non-performance; nor does the fact that the breach can be cured take away the innocent party's right to terminate the contract.[72]   If the innocent party elects to affirm the contract, **both parties** continue to be bound to perform the contract (and the non-performing party has the opportunity to rectify its breach).[73]   It is only if the innocent party elects to terminate the contract that it is discharged from its obligation to perform the contract and is permitted to "withhold" performance.

English law therefore also takes an "all-or-nothing" approach on discharge for breach. Once a repudiatory breach has occurred, the innocent party can only affirm or terminate the contract; there is no middle ground or "third choice"[74] for the innocent party to give the breaching party another opportunity to perform while withholding performance, as Art. 7.1.4 of the Principles permits.   Neither is there an ability for a party to cure a repudiatory breach unilaterally.[75] And as for contract breaches that do not amount to repudiatory breaches, the innocent party's only option is to claim for damages.   Again, the prevailing interests of freedom of contract and certainty of consequences have defined the English approach to avoid imposing any obligation on the innocent party to act in good faith toward the breaching party.

---

[71] See *H. Beale*, Chitty on Contracts, 33d ed., 2018 at [24-002]. In New Zealand, this position has been codified: see Contract and Commercial Law Act 2017, ss. 36-40.

[72] See Buckland v Bournemouth University Higher Education Corporation [2010] EWCA Civ 121, para. 36 ("It is common ground that no decided case holds in terms that a repudiatory breach, once complete … is capable of being remedied so as to preclude acceptance.").

[73] See, e.g., Motor Oil Hellas (Corinth) Refineries SA v Shipping Corporation of India (The Kanchenjunga) [1990] 1 Lloyd's Rep. 391.

[74] See Fercometal SARL v Mediterranean Shipping Co SA [1989] A.C. 788, 801 ("There is no third choice, as a sort of via media, to affirm the contract and yet to be absolved from tendering further performance unless and until [the breaching party] gives reasonable notice that he is once again able and willing to perform.")

[75] Buckland v Bournemouth University Higher Education Corporation [2010] EWCA Civ 121. See also H. Beale, Chitty on Contracts, 33d ed., 2018 at [24-002], fn. 11.

IV. THE UNIDROIT PRINCIPLES AND ENGLISH LAW: GOING FORWARD

The discussion above on the differences between the UNIDROIT Principles and English common law seek to highlight how the underlying assumptions built into English contract law differ from those supporting the UNIDROIT Principles, and to explain why the UNIDROIT Principles may be viewed with hesitation by those with an English common law background. But, in the authors' view, these differences should not be overstated, especially in the context of international commercial practice. Certainly, great strides have been made towards recognizing a general common law principle of good faith in major common law jurisdictions. In *Bhasin v Hrynew*, the Canadian Supreme Court commented that the previous piecemeal approach to good faith lacked certainty or coherence and was out of step with the law of two major trading partners: Québec and the US.[76] Similar debates are taking place in other Commonwealth jurisdictions that are modelled after the English common law,[77] including a line of authority emerging from *Yam Seng*.[78]

Reflecting this trend, there has also been some movement towards the position taken in the UNIDROIT Principles in other areas. Even though pre-contract negotiations and post-contract conduct were historically strictly inadmissible for contract interpretation purposes, as noted above, this rule has been relaxed over time in some jurisdictions; where it applies, such evidence is frequently admitted anyway by the parties' agreement.[79] The potentially harsh effects of the doctrine of frustration have also been recognized.[80] And in the area of

---

[76] Bhasin v Hrynew 2014 SCC 71, para. 41.

[77] See, e.g., Alcatel Australia Ltd v Scarcella (1998) 44 NSWLR 349; Bobux Marketing Ltd v Raynor Marketing Ltd [2001] NZCA 348, paras. 33-46; Ng Giap Hon v Westcomb Securities Pte Ltd [2009] SGCA 19.

[78] See *Leggatt J*, "Contractual Duties of Good Faith", Lecture to the Commercial Bar Association, 18 October 2016, para. 42, citing Globe Motors, Inc v TRW Lucas Varity Electric Steering Ltd [2016] EWCA Civ 396, para. 67.

[79] See, e.g., *R. Goode*, "The Adaptation of English Law to International Commercial Arbitration" (1992) 8(1) Arb. Int'l 1, 6.

[80] See, e.g., National Carriers Ltd v Panalpina (Northern) Ltd [1981] A.C. 675, 707 ("...consideration should be given to whether the English doctrine of frustration

discharge by breach, in finding that there was no right to an opportunity to cure a breach, the English Court of Appeal did so "with some reluctance," acknowledging that the innocent party's unfettered choice as to how to treat the breach despite an offer of cure is "capable of working injustice."[81] All this demonstrates that, while the UNIDROIT Principles may not reflect some aspects of English contract law, they reflect approaches that have been discussed in common law jurisprudence and may, in certain circumstances, even be recognized as the better approach.

Moreover, as Sir Roy Goode has observed, as a common law system, English law is inherently adaptable and *should* adapt to the needs of international commerce.[82] He argues that in international commercial arbitration, English law should account for the international nature of the transaction and be applied having regard to internationally recognized principles and practice. Others have also suggested that domestic law can learn from the UNIDROIT Principles.[83] In short, English common lawyers are becoming more familiar with the concepts underlying the UNIDROIT Principles, and as international trade and commerce increases – especially between parties from different legal traditions – acceptance and use of the UNIDROIT Principles in international commercial contracts is only likely to grow.

On the flipside, the inherent flexibility of the UNIDROIT Principles and their focus on party autonomy should not be forgotten. Parties that are familiar with English law can

---

could be made more flexible…. As often as not there will be an all or nothing situation, the entire loss caused by the frustrating event falling exclusively on one party, whereas justice might require the burden to be shared."). But see *G. Treitel*, Frustration and Force Majeure (3d ed., 2014), para. 15-001, noting that criticisms of English rules on frustration "have not in recent years been frequent or widespread," probably due to the use of express contractual provisions. See also *C. Blake*, "Is A Judicial Discretion Needed to Soften the 'All or Nothing' Nature of the Doctrine of Frustration?" (2015) 2 N.Z. Pub. Int'l. L.J. 76.

[81] Buckland v Bournemouth University Higher Education Corporation [2010] EWCA Civ 121, para. 37. See also White & Carter (Councils) v McGregor [1962] A.C. 413 (Lord Reid), noting that an innocent party should have a legitimate interest in affirming the contract rather than claiming damages.

[82] See *R. Goode*, "The Adaptation of English Law to International Commercial Arbitration" (1992) 8(1) Arb. Int'l 1.

[83] See *P. Finn*, "Symposium Paper: The UNIDROIT Principles: An Australian Perspective" (2010) 17 Austl. Int'l L.J. 193, 196.

construct their agreements in a manner consistent with English law understandings within the ambit of the UNIDROIT Principles. In a nod to English and common law cultures, the Principles' express recognition of merger or entire agreement clauses in Art. 2.1.17 essentially allows parties to agree on the application of the parol evidence rule by expressly excluding evidence of prior statements or agreements from being used to contradict or supplement the terms of a written contract.[84]

In the authors' view, in practice, if parties carefully drew up their agreements with the level of specificity common in English law jurisdictions, there would be little scope for any unpredictable application of the good faith principle and little substantive difference whether the UNIDROIT Principles or English law is the governing law.[85] In other words, the UNIDROIT Principles are entirely consistent with and can accommodate the operation of English contract law principles. At the same time, the Principles also protect parties that are less familiar with English law, with the ability to fill in gaps in a contract in a way that English law may not.

The UNIDROIT Principles are a one-stop, streamlined and coherent body of international contract law. This is itself a major attraction of the UNIDROIT Principles, particularly for parties from legal systems unaccustomed to the precedent-based system of the common law. In addition to being a valuable comparative law resource, the Principles provide an effective option for parties seeking a neutral alternative to a national law. Additionally, the growing recognition of good faith in English law is likely to foster greater acceptance of the Principles generally. This is especially for long term international contracts where civil law meets the common law, including many that will arise from China's Belt and Road Initiative.

---

[84] *See E. Brödermann, UNIDROIT Principles of International Commercial Contracts: An Article-by-Article Commentary* (2018), p. 59.

[85] Broad, untrammeled and unpredictable application of Art. 1.7 is already unlikely due to the existence of detailed provisions in the UNIDROIT Principles specifying how the good faith principle is to be applied: *see* E. Brödermann, *UNIDROIT Principles of International Commercial Contracts: An Article-by-Article Commentary* (2018), pp. 31-32.

CEAC's 10th Anniversary Arbitration Conference on China's Belt and Road Initiative
A Report on the Common and Civil Law Perspectives viz. the Interplay between the UNIDROIT Principles and the CISG

Anish Wadia[*] and Magdalena Göbel[**]

With the intent to preserve the fruitful discussions that took place during CEAC's 10th anniversary conference on China's Belt and Road Initiative, this report summarises Part II of the conference which focused on the possibility of using the UNIDROIT Principles and the CISG to build a bridge between common and civil law in China related contracts. The exceptional diversity of the panels resulted in a structured and informative debate: first, each panelist gave her or his perspective on the use of the UNIDROIT Principles of International Commercial Contracts (UNIDROIT Principles) and the United Nations Convention on Contracts for the International Sale of Goods (CISG), and then, a lively discussion on the interplay between the two, in both theory and practice. In conclusion, all panelists – no matter whether they have regularly used the UNIDROIT Principles in practice or not – shared the view that they could prove to be a helpful tool to build bridges in international contracts, filling gaps existing in other international contract law sources like the CISG. Therefore, the panelists recommended reflection on these Principles' use to all practitioners.

---

[*] Anish Wadia, *FCIArb, FMIArb, FHKIArb, FAIADR, FACICA, FAArb, FCArb, FPIArb, FPD, FAP-KFCRI, FAMINZ (Arb), CFCILS*, is an international arbitrator and lawyer

[**] Magdalena Göbel is a Ph.D. candidate at Bucerius Law School in Hamburg, Germany,

I. Introduction

The middle of September 2018 marked a special occasion for the arbitration world in Hamburg and beyond: The Chinese European Arbitration Center (CEAC) celebrated its 10th anniversary by hosting a conference on China's Belt and Road Initiative and the resulting opportunities and challenges for international dispute resolution and contract drafting. Speakers and participants came together from all around the world to share their views, develop new ideas and expand their network over coffee and drinks while enjoying two beautiful Hanseatic fall days and the breathtaking interiors of the Fairmont Hotel.

CEAC is not merely one amongst the many arbitration institutes which exist around the world, especially when it comes to the Belt and Road Initiative but at the forefront of it. CEAC is the result of the visionary initiative of Professor Dr. Eckart Brödermann[1] and the then Mayor of Hamburg, Ole von Beust, the open exchange between the Hamburg Bar and various Chinese associations and organisations as well as years of travel, preparation and research. Without any of these elements, CEAC could not have been "born", as Dr. Elke Umbeck[2] so aptly put it in a celebratory speech at CEAC's birthday dinner. In fact, the metaphor of childbirth was a recurring motive during the conference, illustrating the tremendous amount of hard work that went into bringing CEAC to its 10th anniversary and a showcase of the hope and determination of all involved to strengthen CEAC so that it may reach adulthood, and beyond.

As China's Belt and Road Initiative relates to both common and civil law jurisdictions, part of the conference was dedicated to discussing the extent to which the UNIDROIT Principles and the

---

[1] Professor Dr. Eckart Brödermann is an honorary Professor at the University of Hamburg, Managing Partner at Brödermann Jahn as well as then honorary Managing Director at CEAC. He has been working in the field of international arbitration for over 30 (thirty) years both as an Arbitrator and Counsel as well as through writing and teaching.

[2] Dr. Elke Umbeck is the Vice President of the Chinese European Legal Association e.V. (CELA) and Chinese European Arbitration Association e.V. (CEAA) as well as a Partner at Heuking Kühn Lüer Wojtek where she co-heads the firm's litigation and arbitration practice group. She is based in Hamburg and regularly acts as Counsel and Arbitrator in national and international proceedings.

CISG can build bridges between these two legal systems – particularly fitting for a CEAC conference because of CEAC's unique model choice of law clause that has proactively referenced and promulgated use of the UNIDROIT Principles.[3] This part of the conference was fittingly moderated by Professor Dr. Anna Veneziano[4], the Deputy Secretary General of the International Institute for the Unification of Private Law (UNIDROIT) together with the author of an UNIDROIT Principles' article-by-article commentary, Prof. Dr. Brödermann.

With the aim to summarise these discussions and to illustrate their outcomes, this report will: (1) describe the benefits of the UNIDROIT Principles as brought forward by the panelists, (2) elucidate the panelists' views on these Principles and the CISG's use in practice, (3) discuss the panelists' answers to the question of whether or not disregarding these rules can lead to a breach of *inter alia* a fiduciary duty, and (4) portray the panelists' opinions on CEAC's model choice of law clause and the possibility of interplay between the UNIDROIT Principles and the CISG.

II. General function of the UNIDROIT Principles

The UNIDROIT Principles, first published in 1994, were designed to harmonise the field of international commercial contract law through a non-legislative codification after the necessary consensus for a binding treaty on the matter could not be achieved. The result of intense preparation by independent experts from all major legal systems is now in its 4th release, the Unidroit Principles of International Commercial Contracts 2016,and the first discussion of the day therefore rightly concentrated on the UNIDROIT Principles' meaning for practitioners.

---

[3] *See*, Article 35 of the CEAC Arbitration Rules.
[4] Professor Dr. Anna Veneziano is the Deputy Secretary General of the International Institute for the Unification of Private Law (UNIDROIT) as well as Professor of Comparative Law at the University of Teramo, Italy.

1. Simplicity of integration and broad scope of application

According to Professor Dr. Jingxia Shi,[5] the first major benefit is the simplicity of utilisation of the UNIDROIT Principles in resolution of international commercial disputes as well as their broad scope of application. She explained that these Principles now encompass all important issues in international contract law and that the solutions they propose have been so well received by both academics and practitioners that numerous court decisions, arbitral awards and even domestic court judgements have referred to these Principles. She further clarified that the UNIDROIT Principles can be used in disputes through three methods of integration, making them extremely easy to apply: (1) they can be chosen as the rule of law governing the dispute, (2) they can be used as a general principle of law on the assumption that they form a common basis of international contract law, or (3) by express consent of the parties in the absence of a choice of law clause or to interpret other applicable law like the CISG in support of a more international approach.

2. Source of inspiration for legislators

Prof. Dr. Shi also drew attention to a second key benefit – role of the UNIDROIT Principles as a source of inspiration for legislators in reforming their state's contract law. This proves to be beneficial in more than one aspect: First, incorporation of these Principles into domestic law ensures their universal application even though technically these Principles are only a soft-law instrument. Second, by taking recourse to these Principles, legislators utilise the carefully researched findings of numerous experts to better adapt their contract law to the needs of international commercial relations and thereby economically advance their country.

---

[5] Professor Dr. Jingxia Shi is the Dean and Professor of International Business and Economic Law at China University of International Business and Economics Law School as well as a member of the Governing Council of the International Institute for the Unification of Private Law (UNIDROIT).

3. Neutral terminology

Another strong point was brought forward by Professor Dr. Stefan Vogenauer[6] who stressed that the availability of the UNIDROIT Principles in virtually all major languages proves to be a vital point in favour of its inclusion at the stage of contract drafting. Even though commercial contracts are often based on templates, which makes incorporating these Principles rather tricky, in his experience, the UNIDROIT Principles are extremely helpful when it comes to contractual terminology. As translating legal terms can be difficult and risky at times, recourse can instead be had to the UNIDROIT Principles' terminology reflecting an international consensus as to the exact meaning of specific legal terms. Further, according to Prof. Dr. Vogenauer, this universal terminology aims to create a degree of balanced neutrality by not using terms specifically assigned to certain legal phenomena in common or civil law jurisdictions.

4. Neutral choice of law

Taking cue from Prof. Dr. Vogenauer's last reference to the neutral language of the UNIDROIT Principles, Prof. Dr. Brödermann pointed out the benefit of and the fact that these Principles also represent a neutral choice of law in general. As Prof. Dr. Brödermann explained, in international contracts, every party will always try to have its law incorporated into the contract. Hence, instead of wasting time with lengthy negotiations that cannot always be "won", he proposed the use of these Principles as a neutral law.

While Professor Dr. Gerhard Wegen[7] disagreed on the usefulness of the UNIDROIT Principles in contracts whose focal

---

[6] Professor Dr. Stefan Vogenauer is the Director of the Max Planck Institute of European Legal History in Frankfurt and former Director of the Oxford Institute of European and Comparative Law as well as the Editor of the Oxford University Press Commentary on the UNIDROIT Principles.

[7] Professor Dr. Gerhard Wegen is a partner at Gleiss Lutz in Stuttgart as well as an honorary professor at the University of Tübingen. Prof. Dr. Wegen regularly participates in international arbitration proceedings both as Arbitrator and Counsel.

point rests in a certain jurisdiction, he endorsed Prof. Dr. Brödermann's proposal of using them in contracts where negotiating every little thing would be too time-consuming, like in commodity contracts or standard commercial contracts. According to Prof. Dr. Wegen, the UNIDROIT Principles' refinement and complexity make them more eligible for use as a governing law or source of inspiration for otherwise applicable domestic law.

Prof. Dr. Veneziano stressed the role of these Principles as a tool in the hands of practitioners, which although not suited to be applied in every dispute might help in many of them. As a result, she concluded that it is highly beneficial for practitioners to know the content of the UNIDROIT Principles to be able to make an informed decision about whether their application would be useful for their clients.

III. Country perspectives on use of the UNIDROIT Principles

The panels were comprised of arbitration experts from multiple jurisdictions including common and civil law educated lawyers. While at first glance their perspectives differed substantively, in the end, they all had similar recommendations echoing Prof. Dr. Veneziano's last remark concerning the general function of the UNIDROIT Principles viz. that lawyers should try to use these Principles and should make sure that they are familiar with their content to provide truly holistic advice in today's global economy.

In getting there, Mr. Roger E. Barton[8] explained that the UNIDROIT Principles, generally speaking, looked very familiar to him as a common law educated lawyer from the United States. He found this especially true with regard to use of the principle of good faith and fair dealing as well as the possibility of modifying a contract through actions by the parties instead of

---

[8] Roger E. Barton is the Founder and Managing Partner of Barton LLP, a US boutique law firm focusing on all areas of business law.

in writing. However, Mr. Barton also stated that these Principles have so far only been used in approximately 33 (thirty-three) cases within the United States and that these cases concerned the possibility of voiding the arbitration clause and litigating in state courts instead of the interpretation of domestic or international law with the help of the UNIDROIT Principles. Usually, the US courts are very strict on that matter and try to uphold the parties' intentions of arbitrating a dispute. However, in his opinion, in an area where a US court does not recognise a UNIDROIT Principle, this can prove to be more of an issue.

Professor M.H. Loutfi[9] added his Egyptian and civil law perspective by illustrating two difficulties: First, he emphasised the issue of limitation periods which are included in the UNIDROIT Principles but non-existent in Islamic law countries. Second, he reminded the participants that the concept of penalties is foreign to civil law which requires a discernable damage as prerequisite for any compensation.

Further issues were then addressed by Ms. Dharshini Prasad,[10] who pertinently pointed out that even within common law countries there might not be a consensus regarding the UNIDROIT Principles. Drawing from her transnational expertise, Ms. Prasad exemplified that while the principle of good faith and the use of pre-contractual negotiations is very much familiar to lawyers from the United States, their use is highly contentious in the United Kingdom and in Singapore. Bearing that in mind, Ms. Prasad nevertheless argued that these Principles could be valuable in assisting courts to give a more accurate interpretation of contracts. In conclusion, she submitted that the UNIDROIT Principles should be used when possible.

---

[9] Professor Mohamed-Hossam Loutfi is the Professor of Civil Law at Beni-Suef University, Egypt, as well as an Attorney-at-Law and owner of Loutfi Law Firm in Egypt. He has been involved in arbitration since 1983 both as an Arbitrator and Counsel. Mr. Loutfi co-authored the Arabic version of three editions of the UNIDROIT Principles 1994, 2004 and 2010.

[10] Ms. Dharshini Prasad is an attorney in the international arbitration group of Wilmer Cutler Pickering Hale and Dorr LLP in London where she focuses on complex multi-jurisdictional disputes advising states, state entities and multi-national companies on commercial, investment and international law issues.

Prof. Dr. Wegen added another issue specifically from a German law context: In German state courts a choice of law clause incorporating privately agreed law, like the UNIDROIT Principles, instead of state law will be considered not as a valid choice of law but as mere incorporation of such soft law.[11] While this is not true for arbitral proceedings, Prof. Dr. Wegen still advised practitioners to keep this in mind and check conflict rules in the specific jurisdiction before choosing these Principles in contracts to avoid being surprised by the law that would ultimately be applied.

IV. Country perspectives on use of the CISG

The panelists also expressed their different perspectives on the use of the CISG which – although an international treaty with binding force – has been received differently in different jurisdictions around the world. While parties from some countries, like China, embraced its content from the very beginning, parties from other countries, like Germany and the United States, have automatically opted out within their contracts.

Professor Dr. Ingeborg Schwenzer[12] illustrated the potential dangers of such an automatic exclusion, especially if the consequence were, for example, to choose Swiss law as a presumed neutral law without really knowing its content. Swiss law is the second most chosen law in the world even though, according to Prof. Dr. Schwenzer, it is not equipped for international cases and is highly unpredictable due to a lack of precedents by the Swiss Supreme Court with regard to to many issues. However, the wish to opt out of the CISG may have its

---

[11] Note from the editors: See Rome I Regulation on the law applicable to contractual obligations (EU O.J. 2008 L 177, p. 6), Recital no. 13 and Gerhard Wegen´s article-by-acticle commentary of substantial parts of the Rome I-Regulation, co-authored with one of the editors, in Prütting/Wegen/Weinreich (ed.), BGB Kommentar (13th edition 2018), IPR-Anh 1/ROM I no. 4, at p. 3321-3322.

[12] Professor Dr. Ingeborg Schwenzer is the Dean of the Swiss International Law School and Professor emerita of Private Law at the University of Basel, Switzerland, as well as the Editor and main contributor of the world's leading commentary on the Convention on the International Sale of Goods.

reasons: Mr. Angelo Anglani[13] pointed out that lawyers might not have the necessary expertise when it comes to the CISG and may feel more comfortable to refer to known domestic rules when drafting a contract even though this might, in principle, turn out to be a worse choice. In his opinion, an additional factor is the need for supplementation of the CISG as it does not cover all contract law issues. He explained that this creates uncertainty regarding the question on which areas will be supplemented and by what. On that note, he reasoned that a lot would depend on the correct application of the CISG by the responsible judge, who at times might be as unfamiliar with the CISG as many lawyers. Avoiding these risks is one reason for parties to opt out, which is not an aspect that can be tackled by the CISG itself. Another reason – at least where German parties are concerned – used to be that German sales law was more beneficial for sellers in the past and, as a result, most of the parties from the exporting nation of Germany opted out of the CISG's application to enjoy the benefits of their domestic law. However, as Prof. Dr. Brödermann observed, parties forgot to change their ways after the 2002 reform of German sales law. Germany's new sales law is not only to a large extent identical to the CISG but also includes strict consumer protection provisions, which, in his opinion, can and should be avoided in business to business contracts in the interests of sellers by opting for the CISG.

From countries with a higher use of the CISG, Mrs. Anna Grishchenkova[14], from the Russian perspective, stated that the CISG is very well known, parties usually don't opt out and even Russian courts are generally well aware of its content. Prof. Dr. Shi added that in China, the CISG will automatically apply between parties whose states of origin are part of the convention, unless they expressly opt out. Prof. Dr. Shi also explained that the CISG takes precedence over Chinese law in international disputes. In general, the CISG has had a very profound influence on the Chinese legal system, from lawyers to

---

[13] Mr. Angelo Anglani is a Partner at Nctm Studio Legale in Rome, Italy, focusing on cross border litigation and international arbitration.

[14] Mrs. Anna Grishchenkova is a Partner at KIAP Attorneys-at-law in Moscow, Russia, focusing on international arbitration, as well as the co-editor and co-author of the Commentary on Russian Arbitration Laws by the Russian Arbitration Association.

government officials to legal education. According to Prof. Dr. Shi, this influence was also strongly felt in the legislative field, as is underlined by the fact that the 1999 Chinese contract law is derived in large parts from the CISG.

Thereafter, the Brazilian perspective – a country that only recently joined the CISG – was elucidated by Professor Dr. Lauro Gama Jr.[15] who underlined the CISG's importance and further the openness of Brazilian courts towards the application of international law in general, be it the CISG or the UNIDROIT Principles. This openness reached so far as to a Brazilian court of appeal inviting the Danish and Brazilian parties to use the CISG even though the contract had been concluded before Brazil ratified it, as the judges felt a transnational legal system like the CISG would best govern this international relationship.[16]

V. Failure to consider the UNIDROIT Principles as a breach of fiduciary duty

In his continued fiercely passionate logical endeavour to illustrate to practitioners the necessity of applying the UNIDROIT Principles, Prof. Dr. Brödermann put an interesting question up for debate: As the UNIDROIT Principles restate, at least to some degree, universally accepted principles of international contract law, would their simple disregard not lead to a breach of every company manager's or advising lawyer's fiduciary duty to minimise risks in contracts?

Mr. Barton quickly agreed that the fiduciary duty obliges managers and lawyers to also look at the UNIDROIT Principles and Prof. Dr. Schwenzer even mentioned that counsel could be

---

[15] Professor Dr. Lauro Gama, Jr., is a founding partner of Lauro Gama Attorneys in Rio di Janeiro, Brazil, focusing on international arbitration, as well as an adjunct professor of law at Pontifical Catholic University of Rio di Janeiro where he teaches Private International Law, Contracts, Arbitration and International Business Transactions. He also participated in the working group of the UNIDROIT Principles and was a member of the CISG Advisory Council.

[16] *Noridane Foods S.A. v/s Anexo Comercial Importação e Distribuição Ltda*, Court of Appeal of Rio Grande do Sul, 14 February 2017, Case No. 70072362940.

held liable for excluding the CISG without knowing its content. However, Prof. Dr. Wegen had doubts viz. the transferability of such a liability in CISG cases to cases involving the UNIDROIT Principles. Unlike Mr. Barton and Prof. Dr. Schwenzer, he argued that the CISG is a public international law treaty and therefore, part of the law of the respective state which cannot be disregarded. To the converse of the CISG, he added that the UNIDROIT Principles are soft-law, whose application is voluntary. Prof. Dr. Wegen advised considering all applicable laws in the best interest of the client, but argued that so far, he would not consider disregarding of the UNIDROIT Principles a breach of a fiduciary duty. Yet, he stated that this might change one day.

Concerning the duty of corporate managers, Prof. Dr. Shi followed Prof. Dr. Brödermann's notion more closely and argued in favor of an obligation to take the UNIDROIT Principles into account. However, she convincingly raised the issue that even though such an obligation may be argued, bringing forth an intentional violation would be difficult bearing in mind the burden of proof.

With regard to the future development of this issue, Prof. Dr. Veneziano spoke about a comprehensive research project by the International Bar Association, focusing on the practical implications of the UNIDROIT Principles and the evaluation of cases to determine whether or not a better suited result could have been achieved using these Principles. The outcome of this project could potentially lead to a better understanding in how far lawyers and company managers can be obliged to take the UNIDROIT Principles into account. [17]

---

[17] *See*, 'IBA partners with UNIDROIT to harmonise global contract law' <https://www.ibanet.org/news-analysis-august-september-2018.aspx#3> accessed 09 October 2018.

VI. Article 35 of the CEAC Rules – interplay between the UNIDROIT Principles and the CISG

After having discussed the use of the UNIDROIT Principles and the CISG respectively, the last point of discussion concentrated on the choice of law provision contained in Article 35(1) of the CEAC Rules, which, in a nutshell, provides three options: domestic law, the CISG supplemented by the UNIDROIT Principles or the UNIDROIT Principles supplemented by otherwise applicable law.[18] This unique model clause thereby explicitly references not only the UNIDROIT Principles as the applicable law but also already proposes an interplay between these Principles and the CISG.

In that regard, Professor Dr. Bruno Zeller[19] astutely advised that when making a choice, lawyers and company managers should know why they choose that specific law and which risks they wish to cover by opting for such law. That said, he endorsed the options included in Article 35 of the CEAC Rules, as they give parties the opportunity of choosing a neutral law like the CISG supplemented not by subjective domestic law but by another set of neutral rules like the UNIDROIT Principles.

In discussing the practicability of such an interplay between the two, Prof. Dr. Schwenzer pointed to the issue of contradictory provisions in the CISG and the UNIDROIT Principles, where a supplementation could prove not only difficult but impossible. She mentioned Article 78 of the CISG which provides for interest payments without setting an interest rate and Article 7.4.9 of the UNIDROIT Principles which includes an elaborate rule on interest payments including a determination of rates. Prof. Dr. Schwenzer argued that although the CISG lacks a provision in this regard, such a gap should not be filled with the UNIDROIT Principles as this issue was intentionally left open to allow parties from Arab countries, where interest rates are prohibited, to use the CISG without reservations. Moreover, she

---

[18] *See*, 'Model Clause' <https://www.ceac-arbitration.com/arbitration/model-clauses/choice-of-law-clause> accessed 09 October 2018.

[19] Professor Dr. Bruno Zeller is the Professor of Transnational Commercial Law at the University of Western Australia in Crawley, Australia.

explained that while using a strict liability approach at first glance, the UNIDROIT Principles differentiate between obligations of means and obligations of result and thereby, let a civil law approach of different degrees of fault creep in through the back door.

However, Prof. Dr. Gama Jr. convincingly distinguished between supplementing what he called internal and external gaps: the CISG internal gaps are areas that are covered but not governed by it – such as hardship, the fixing of interest rates and limitation periods, and, the CISG external gaps are areas not covered by the CISG at all – such as the substantive validity of the contract, plurality of obligors and obligees and assignments of rights and obligations. Prof. Dr. Schwenzer agreed regarding this last point in stating that a supplementation could be a good approach concerning such real gaps within the CISG. However, Prof. Dr. Gama Jr. concluded that the UNIDROIT Principles play a very important role in both scenarios, as the risk of contradictory provisions is small, and the basic underlying principles of both instruments are quite similar. Where in internal gaps the UNIDROIT Principles can help to modernise and develop the CISG, in external gaps the UNIDROIT Principles provide practitioners, judges and arbitrators with modern rules of an international character that are usually apt to govern every type of international sales transaction.

Prof. Dr. Gama Jr. subsequently went much further with his line of argument, explaining that, contrary to Prof. Dr. Schwenzer's hopes, filling the CISG's gaps by new proposals of the CISG advisory council will ultimately fail. In his opinion, as the CISG is a hard-law instrument, finding a new consensus among the now 89 (eighty-nine) contracting states will be practically impossible. Additionally, he emphasised the importance of recognising the growing body of soft-law instruments governing a wide variety of issues from banking to criminal to tax law, concluding that their normative character is not negligible any longer. As a result, he proposed to take not only the UNIDROIT Principles into account when supplementing and modernising the CISG, but also other soft-law to gradually update international law.

VII.   Concluding Remarks

Prof. Dr. Shi stressed the most important aspect of the UNIDROIT Principles when it comes to their future: The possibility to adapt to new developments. These Principles can be updated much easier than the CISG can be revised. Upon request of the UNIDROIT Governing Council, legal and business communities can be consulted to see if proposed new principles should be added like it was done in the most recent release 2016 with regard to long-term contracts. In doing so, Prof. Dr. Shi concluded that so far, the UNIDROIT Principles have succeeded in bridging the gap between common and civil law by adding principles that are new to both legal regimes but solve existing problems occurring in one or the other legal regime. Similarly, Prof. Dr. Veneziano underscored that the winning aspect of the UNIDROIT Principles has always been that they were aimed at solving practical issues by having experts from numerous jurisdictions with diverse backgrounds and practical experience, at the table. Further, and due to the optional nature of the UNIDROIT Principles, a factor that was also greatly emphasised by Prof. Dr. Veneziano and Prof. Dr. Brödermann, Prof. Dr. Shi argued that it will always be possible to include both: provisions that are already widely recognised as well as new ideas that appeal to the international business world. In her view, this key benefit of the UNIDROIT Principles demonstrates how they can one day fully fulfil their role as a universal regulator of international trade with high credibility.

Contributing Authors

Roger E. Barton
Roger E. Barton, Esq. is the Managing Partner of Barton LLP in New York City
rbarton@bartonesq.com

Magdalena Göbel
is a Ph.D. candidate at Bucerius Law School in Hamburg, Germany
magdalena.goebel@law-school.de

Benedikt Keil
Benedikt Keil is trainee lawyer, GLEISS LUTZ, Stuttgart (Germany)
benedikt.keil@gleisslutz.com

Markus Kotzur
Prof. Dr. Markus Kotzur is Vice Dean of the Law Faculty of the University of Hamburg
markus.kotzur@uni-hamburg.de

Dharshini Prasad
Senior Associate, Wilmer Cutler Pickering Hale and Dorr LLP
Dharshini.Prasad@wilmerhale.com

Rina See
is Counsel, Wilmer Cutler Pickering Hale and Dorr LLP
Rina.See@wilmerhale.com

Anish Wadia
Anish Wadia, Solicitor Advocate, Arbitrator & Counsel is an international arbitrator and lawyer
a.wadia@anishwadia.com

Gerhard Wegen
Prof. Dr. Gerhard Wegen is Partner, GLEISS LUTZ, Stuttgart (Germany), LL.M. (Harvard)
gerhard.wegen@gleisslutz.com

Bruno Zeller
Dr. Bruno Zeller is a Professor of Transnational Law in the Law School at the University of Western Australia, Perth
bruno.zeller@uwa.edu.au

Hamburg Law Review
Journal of the Law Faculty at the University of Hamburg

Editors-in-Chief
Prof. Dr. Eckart Brödermann
eckart.broedermann@uni-hamburg.de
Prof. Dr. Hinrich Julius
hinrich.julius@jura.uni-hamburg.de
Prof. Dr. Dr. h.c. Marian Paschke
marian.paschke@jura.uni-hamburg.de

Editorial Assistance for Issue 2018/2
Prof. Dr. Eckart Brödermann
Prof. Dr. Dr. h.c. Marian Paschke

Student Editors
Clara-Sophie Groß

Editorial Office
Jasmin Neumann
jasmin.neumann@jura.uni-hamburg.de

Subscription Information for the Journal
ISBN print edition 978-3-7494-9295-4
ISBN electronic edition 978-3-7494-0241-0

ISSN 2511-3933

Electronic Edition
An electronic edition of this journal is available
at most European online stores

Orders and Inquiries worldwide at any book store or at
University of Hamburg
Faculty of Law
HLR-Office, Ms. Jasmine Neumann
Rothenbaumchaussee 33
20148 Hamburg
Tel.: +49 (0)40 42838 5995
Fax: +49 (0)40 42838 4546
Email: jasmin.neumann@uni-hamburg.de
URL: http://www.jura.uni-hamburg.de

Price of this volume EUR 9,80. This issue is also available incl. shipment worldwide for EUR 28 at the place of production:
Books on Demand GmbH
In de Tarpen 42
22848 Norderstedt
Tel.: +49 40 - 53 43 35 80
Fax: +49 40 - 53 43 35 84
Email: joerg.zaag@bod.de
URL: www.bod.de